Forward

My first idea to write a book came at an early age. My title was *Man in the Basement*, and it would be a book about man's struggle for happiness. It was never written until now.

I've discovered that many people are not happy with their lives. I'm one of those people things happen to, so my sister-in-law told me I should write a book. My life is about the struggle for happiness (as it is for most people, I guess). We all chase rainbows and dreams, but so few of us discover happiness. Only after a series of challenges, always being in the pursuit of material things, and ultimately adopting a minimalistic lifestyle, did I—then and only then—finally discover happiness.

This book also reflects on life in the Florida Keys, and my addiction to sitting underneath a palm tree, essentially doing nothing as much as possible.

I hope this book encourages other people to focus on sunsets instead of granite countertops.

Thank-yous

I want to thank Susan Rauscher for giving me advice on my story line and editing.

Thank you to my friend Brandy for telling me her story about growing up as the daughter of a Florida crab fisherman—it was the final push to get me to write (I hope she writes her story one day).

Thank you to my sister-in-law for encouraging me to write my story. Thank you to my parents for all those wonderful years in the Florida Keys, and everything they did for me. I also want to acknowledge my friend Patti, from my hometown, for encouraging me to stick my neck out and not worry about the opinions of other people.

Also, a special thank you to the Gladwell family for all those wonderful years at Big Pine Key Fishing Lodge.

Dedication

To Patty in New Hampshire who showed me the path to happiness.

1

Living in a small town...is like living in a large family of rather uncongenial relations. Sometimes it's fun, and sometimes it's perfectly awful, but it's always good for you. People in large towns are like only-children.

— Joyce Dennys

My earliest significant memory comes from a time when I was six years old. I was playing in my hometown, Caledonia, with a friend. We were crawling up a cement ledge, not a parent in sight. It was a time when the older kids were expected to take care of the younger kids, and kids stayed outside until the streetlights came on. I was struggling to keep up with my friend and I reached for a weed that was not strong enough to hold me. I dropped to the ground below, a good five-foot drop, and split open my chin. Landing on my face was certainly not my plan! I remember hearing my neighbour, who had witnessed my fall, scream at the amount of blood pouring from my face. It was like a clip from a horror film. I made my way home and, after the removal of two small stones and the addition of a few stitches, life carried on.

Looking back at the amount of unsupervised play, I'm surprised more kids didn't get seriously hurt. It was a different time. Helicopter Parenting had not been invented yet—kids wandered, fathers worked, and many women of that era were still somewhat trapped in their homes, perhaps with a large bottle of vodka under the sink to "get mother through the day." Still, I made it through the summer without further incident or injury.

My next memory takes place in the fall. I remember how important it was to me, at the time, to avoid the expansion cracks in the sidewalk. "Step on a crack, break your momma's back," I chanted, hopping over the lines. I dragged my hands across the concrete retaining walls until my fingers burned; I left white, dusty handprints. Cold sunshine made dancing stars on the river. I wiped my snot on my sleeve, wishing I had mittens. I looked up into the bright sun and I saw those little seahorses—the floaters

(I wondered what those things were...). I also got them when I sneezed. So many questions. So many thoughts go through your mind when you are young.

I was walking downtown on a shopping run for my parents, although I don't remember what for. My parents were always entertaining and I was often sent out for forgotten items. For some reason, I found myself in a long line. It seems that the Santa Claus parade had ended, and I had missed it. My European parents had informed me that Santa was not real over a year ago, so obviously I was not going to be a spectator at the annual parade, was I? Still, how lucky was I to find myself at the end of the line with other eager kids for a handout of post-parade candy?! Finally, after waiting a long time, I was at the front of the line. The volunteer had a grey mustache and wrinkled eyes: weirdly coloured blue eyes that reminded me of my neighbour's dog. The basket into which he reached was empty. In the frenzied handouts, they had run out. He looked at me and said, "Sorry, kid, we're out of candy." Then he reached into his pocket and drew out a quarter. I took it, but I was so disappointed. I left the empty parking lot and headed home. I always felt that life wasn't going to be easy.

2

Men talk of killing time, while time quietly kills them.

– Dion Boucicault

It was hot out, and I was sweating in the back seat of my father's truck; we didn't have air conditioning. My grandfather refused to open the passenger window. He was wearing a thin sweater and neatly pressed pants, and he felt cold in the way old people often do. My grandfather talked to my father while listening to his favourite classical music station. He leaned toward the speaker instead of asking for the volume to be turned up. He needed to feel the music.

The sun was shining brightly through the window, lighting up the particles of dust that floated about our heads. He carried our surname with him from his home country, Latvia. Translated to English, it means "beam of light." I stared at the backs of their heads and thought that one day I would be the driver, with my father next to me and my grandfather gone.

As a young man, my grandfather worked for the Ministry of Employment, and was awarded for his role in stopping the overthrow of his country. He lived a good life in Riga, with a good job, a government apartment, and a lovely wife and son. I never got to meet my grandmother, as she died of tuberculosis at the age of forty. My father's life was turned upside down shortly thereafter when the Germans occupied their city.

My grandfather fled to Sweden; he was one of the lucky ones who got out. He never did get over the death of his wife. Some would say that he gave up on life, really, and sort of drifted in his existence. I think it's true that some people never get over a loss.

When he came to Canada, he mostly lived with family. He was a charismatic and engaging man who wore people out, but he always found his way back into their good graces. When my father and mother came to Canada, they put him into an apartment and took good care of him.

My grandfather was a natural performer and was an amateur actor with the Latvian community in Cleveland and Toronto. By North American standards, you might consider my grandfather lazy. He had all that talent but spent his life as a dishwasher. He never cared much about money. Was it laziness, a lack of drive, or did he have it right, even back then? Is laziness hereditary? I wonder. There are days when I would like to lay a blanket across my legs like an old man and just sit.

Oh, how he loved the orchestra! He listened to Carmen, and he once cried at a guitar rendition of Volga Boatman that I played. He was sentimental that way. He loved to visit his sister and drink cognac and vodka and reminisce about the old days. Over time, he turned into a shadow of the man he once was. He fell asleep in his chair without remembering how he got there. He pounded the floor with a bat to get his daughter-in-law's attention so she could help him to the bathroom. It wasn't long before my parents broke the news to him: he would have to go to an old age home. The days that once stretched out ahead of him became shorter. I visited him in the hospital, hugged him, and kissed him on the cheek. We laughed because the masks made it tricky. It was to be my last visit with him; our final goodbye. Thirty-nine years after his death, I retraced his steps and follow his memories to Kuldiga, Latvia. I need to see it for myself, because the one thing I've learned is that life is short.

3

I never had any friends later on like the ones I had when I was twelve, Jesus, does anyone?
– Richard Stephen Dreyfuss in *Stand By Me*.

When I was a kid, I belonged to a gang that we dubbed "The General War Club." We were keen when we first formed our club; we settled on a dues structure and appointed a leader. This was serious business—to us, anyway.

We were a diverse group, to be sure. We had the "Fat Kid" in our gang, a short little Dutch boy with a round face who looked like his mom. His mom hated me because, in her eyes, I was trouble! We had one really smart guy in our group whose parents were academics, and he was heading down the same path in life.

"The Loner" was more mature than the rest of us. I was the one who had the idea to form the club, so I was "The Organizer." Dues were ten cents per member and the Dutch kid was in charge of the money. He kept it in a metal box. We had no plan for the money, but it seemed right to collect it anyway; it was our idea of what people in clubs do.

We used to slide down a coal chute at the academic kid's house. There was a little door at the side of the house that we would climb through, one at a time, then slide down and land in the basement, covered in a cloud of coal dust. I would come home black as black.

We spent a lot of time discussing serious, deep subjects—things like religion, and the Cold War. We shared the opinions of our parents, mimicked the grown-up conversations we'd overheard at home, and came to the mutual conclusion that Russians were bad. We talked about God and all sorts of weird shit.

My opinions about God and religion were not well developed. My parents were atheists and so, by association, was I. Once, I was tricked by my friend's parents into going to a Catholic service. How is that possible, you ask? Well, I thought I was going over to play hockey, but instead they dragged me to church. The priest asked me if I was confirmed, to which I replied, "Here!" That's how much I knew about religion, ritual, and sacrament . . . He mumbled a few words at me and I was good to go! He could keep his blessing as far as I was concerned; it held no significance for me.

The club, which had started off with a bang of enthusiasm and good intentions, ended up having no meaning, really, and after three weeks, the dues were in arrears and we got tired of sliding down the coal chute. There was no formal "disbanding" of the gang, and there were no hard feelings between us; we just lost interest in the formality of it all.

Several years later, we formed a new gang, this time with no name, no dues, and no structure beyond designating "The Loner" as our leader. We were brought together by a love of adventure and a mutual desire to explore and make sense of the world, and were given all the freedom to do so. We rode our bikes to Boston Creek, located near the Gypsum plant.

We all had chopper bikes with banana seats and cardboard jammed into our spokes for noise. The "Fat Kid" had streamers on his bike (streamers were for girls, but we didn't tell him that). The banana seats looked cool but made riding on the shoulder rough. We rode on the side of a highway, which sounds dangerous, but there was a lot less traffic in those days.

We played in the creek and caught live crayfish. We ended up cooking them on an open fire, the other boys not certain if they were edible. We threw "dare you" and "bet you" taunts at each other. With my Scandinavian background (my mom was from Norway), I knew that the crayfish would be good, and I won that bet, hands down.

The talk turned once more to current events. We were worried about something called "acid rain." "What is it, do you think?" we asked each other. "Is it like the Love Canal?" Such big topics, delivered to our young brains via the evening news.

Later in the day, we dropped our bikes in a field by an abandoned train caboose. We talked about making this our clubhouse. Much to our surprise, we found evidence that our clubhouse already had an occupant—an old copy of *Playboy*. My eyes popped!

We didn't have smokes, but we talked about trying them. I rolled cigarettes on a regular basis in the kitchen with my mom, so I had easy access. I thought about how I could filch one for the next time we met. Then, just as things were going so great, the father of "The Loner" found us, and he was furious. We scattered and rode our bikes home. It had been an awesome day. We didn't see "The Loner" for quite some time after that. I'm so glad to have grown up in a small, rural town. I feel like small town living is just better for kids than city living.

4

Most of the time, a kid doesn't think about what he's doing or why. This is the privilege of childhood.
— Robert Fulghum

It's Kindergarten, and I'm singing. It was a full action song, one I'm sure you're familiar with:

> *She'll be comin' 'round the mountain, when she comes (stomp, stomp, clap clap)*

> *She'll be comin' 'round the mountain, when she comes (stomp, stomp, clap clap)*

She'll be comin' 'round the mountain, she'll be comin' 'round the mountain

She'll be comin' 'round the mountain, when she comes (stomp, stomp, clap clap)

Well, the last verse was more like: stomp, stomp, clap, clap, PLOP! I was trying to hold it, I promise, but there it was—a fresh landmine hit the floor. I hid my shame behind a door.

My brother was called out of grade seven to take me home. There I was, the little brother, starving for attention; it shaped my life and personality. I walked up the hill, legs apart. My brother, who hated school, thanked me profusely and begged me to shit myself every day . . .

In the hospital where I was born, I was given the nicknames "Cabbage Boy" and "Stinky." These aren't the most attractive of nicknames and they were obviously not indicative of how damn cute I was, which is proven to be true as I was named "Baby of the Month" in the Hamilton Mountain News.

For some reason, people like to give me nicknames. In Florida, it seems everyone has a nickname, as I would later learn. I earned the nickname "Can Opener" after I fell off of a bridge and chipped my tooth. I also got "Motor Mouth" for, well, the obvious reason. I do love to talk and it's both a blessing and a curse. My father called me "drit sak," which is Swedish for "shit bag." There's an acceptable amount of cruelty in European parenting, and my father would have sworn that his choice of nickname was "character building."

Starzy is a nickname that stuck, and it's a nickname that I like.

Yes, I was the annoying little brother. I wanted so desperately to play with my older brother, and wanted him to *want* to play with me! Who wants to play with someone who's five years younger? Well, my brother and his friends were playing darts in the mud room, ignoring me, so I ran right into the line of fire. My brother, who had been aiming for a bull's eye, got a Carl's eye instead. My mother freaked out, removed the dart from my eye (a first aid no-no, by the way), and rushed me to the doctor. I was declared injury free, and damn lucky.

A few weeks later, at breakfast, as boys will, my brother and I were spitting cherry pits at each other across the table. The game was this: my brother spit a cherry pit at me and I had to catch it in my mouth. We were making a big mess and I was tired of the game and the abuse when my brother insisted that we try one more time. He shot out a pit and it came at me like a torpedo! From five feet away, this cherry pit shot up my nose and stuck. It was a one in a million shot! My mother dug around up there with toothpicks, but the damn thing wouldn't come out. And then, a miracle: a sneeze blew it out and it was airborne once again. This brought a lot of laughter and became a typical "Carl Story" to add to the collection.

I have so many memories from my childhood. I remember when my brother cleaned his gun in the living room and shot out the picture tube of our television set. My brother had to work to pay the repairman; a lesson in responsibility, early in life. I learned that my brother was a good shot!

My mother waited on us hand and foot when we were sick; like a nurse in a sanatorium or hospice. I remember my brother once threw his snot rag at my mom; it landed behind her glasses and she almost dropped her serving tray. Who uses a serving tray anymore? Where have they all gone?

I remember being in grade two on Valentine's Day. I was pleading for help to complete my Valentine's cards (that we were told we had to send), and I asked my mother, "How do you spell 'from'?" She spelled it out for me, and I diligently and painstakingly filled out twenty-three cards that read: "FORM CARL." This is what undiagnosed dyslexia looks like! When my neighbour bought an old Chrysler that was in need of constant repair, I called it a "melon."

I also had a quirky understanding of things: I thought my brother Hans and I had designated water taps (H and C for Hans and Carl); I watched the evening news and heard about the market price of gold and wondered why everyone was so concerned about the cost of soup (bullion not bouillon); and I heard that monkeys (Guerillas) were fighting humans in a foreign country—who gave them the guns and how did they learn how to shoot?

Despite my dyslexia and my strange way of interpreting things, I got good grades. So good, in fact, that I was able to graduate one semester early and take an early three-month holiday to the Florida Keys. This, my friends, is when I discovered paradise.

5

No one is free, even the birds are chained to the sky.

— Bob Dylan

Neighbourhoods change. Two of the families from behind and beside us left, taking their fourteen kids with them. Luckily, two more boys moved in close by, and I became friends with the younger one. His family moved from the wrong side of town, so I thought. They were from the city.

The leaves were a really dark green, but somehow, I knew fall could come quick. Summers don't last long enough when you are ten. The Grand River had been diverted to a large moat and the construction of the dam was about to begin. The river claimed one life per year on average. It seemed that visitors from Hamilton were most susceptible to drowning.

My friends and I took our rods and fished for carp with cans of corn or cornmeal, and molasses balls. It seemed too easy. In a short time, we caught many eight-pound carp. Caught them and let them go, of course, because you didn't want to eat a carp (Canadians didn't, but my European father smoked them in a smoker in our backyard, I just didn't want my friends to know). It was fun, but the thrill left us when, after a few hours, we realized we were catching the same fish over and over.

I left the gang to go fish somewhere else, by myself, which I liked. I was doing fine alone, and I thought I would fish for a while longer, then go home to greet my dad as he came home from work. He was a truck driver and did runs to North Bay all the time.

The kids in the group were mad that I didn't stay with them. The older guy in the group had a pellet gun and he fired off a pellet that whizzed by my ear. The second pellet was a million-dollar shot that pinged off the tin can of fish hooks that I had stuffed in my back pocket. I ran my gear home and returned to the group, hoping that they had found a better target to aim at.

Thankfully, my tin "ass can" had given them the idea to do some real target shooting. And while that was fun enough, someone got the idea that we should shoot a bird.

I remember it being so sunny. The wind had picked up so the breeze seemed to push the water over the dam. The water was brown with the mud churned up from the bottom; nature's chocolate fountain. The whirlpool was powerful and could take you quickly, so we were cautious.

On a small rock at the top of the dam, sat a red-winged blackbird. We took turns, trying to get as close to the bird as possible and take a shot. The bird would raise itself slightly, but always returned to the same spot. It seemed to be fighting to stay in that place, and I imagined that it was enjoying the view and the moment, and that's why it refused to fly away. The truth is, it was injured in the first few shots and couldn't fly away. My last shot tipped the bird over into the whirlpool where it was lost.

Initially, we were euphoric and shouted with glee. But, quite suddenly, we were struck by what we'd done. There was no reason to kill the bird. The bird's markings symbolized strength and bravery; we knew that they, by nature, didn't fear anything, especially when they were protecting a nesting mate.

I always regretted killing that bird. I am not alone in experiencing the regrets of childhood. Every time I see a red-winged blackbird, it reminds me of my crime.

How odd these memories seem as I age, and how I am reminded, once again, that in life, time is short.

6

Fishing is like street fighting. Someone always has a bigger fish. Someone is always tougher.

— Carl Stars

Reflecting on my childhood, I realize just how darn cool my parents were. They worked super hard, and although some of the things we did were not "normal" to others, our family adventures were normal to us.

As Europeans, my parents valued holidays. They always seemed to have money for vacations, while our neighbours didn't seem to go anywhere. They first came to Canada in 1957 and a year later had already taken a trip to Saskatchewan. The floor of my dad's car was rotten and my mother got tired of looking at the yellow line on the road through the hole in the floor. Some chicken wire and poured concrete and my parents had a new car floor and were headed west.

My parents were incredibly resourceful. My father once saw a headline in the paper that indicated someone who worked at a local fuel company had died in a car accident. My father was at the fuel company the next morning asking if they were hiring. In a short time, he was delivering coal just like he was when he lived in Sweden where he had met my mother.

One year, my father bought a school bus. Yes, a full-sized school bus. He bought it for $800, brought it home, and painted it red. The bus had plywood bench seats and homemade curtains. It even had room for a small dining table and a cooktop, where my mother prepared meals. Dad left the original number on the bus, and it was once recognized in Stoney Lake by its original driver who'd driven it for twenty years! He even drove it to work on occasion. That night my dad drove it to work I would have been embarrassed, My parents never cared what people thought and that's why they were happy and successful.

Even before we had crossed the railroad tracks outside of our town, I was asking, "How many more miles until we're there?" I was that kid.

The stick shift was worn through with use; silver showed through the black paint where the bus driver's hand had rested for years. My father's fingers wore away the rest of the paint to help pass the time, as the bus hummed and vibrated as he drove. Many hours into our trip, my mom invented games to alleviate the boredom that kids inevitably feel on a long journey. We played "punch buggy," and counted roadkill. Monopoly was a challenge, as the hotels kept sliding off the board. But we tried anyway.

At night we slept on a bunk bed that dropped down over the table at the back. My parents often entertained fellow travellers at that table; cigarette smoke and mosquito coil vapours mixing into some noxious concoction that drifted into our young lungs. Agent Orange party camper...

My dad was happy on the way up north. Even though he had already spent all week as a professional driver, driving to our holiday destination gave him pleasure. He sang "Moon River" and "Harbour Lights" as we cruised down the highway.

We had given up having pets after once losing our family cat, Sam. He left us at West Lake to find a mate, and we never saw him again. We travelled far too much to have pets; it was a sacrifice that we were willing to make, as our trips were epic.

We reached our destination—a place called Nagagamisis. My dad and I went fishing and I hooked a large northern pike. It was heavy and had a lot of fight in it, which made capturing it even harder for a little kid like me. My dad coached me into landing it, and his help, plus the trophy size of this fish, made me feel more important than my brother. The fish weighed nine and a half pounds, and I bragged to the whole camp about it. At the fish cleaning table, I was momentarily devastated to learn that another fisherman had caught a ten pounder. It was humbling.

In the camper, my Norwegian mother would grind up the fish and fry up fiske kaka (fish patties in Norwegian) on the stove. She would share them with the neighbours, and they disappeared fast! I like them cold even better.

I was so excited to eat the fish I'd caught, and, in the excitement, I loaded my plate with potato salad. After one bite, I found I didn't care for it. My father forced me to eat it all, to punish me for my gluttony. In that instant, my father went from hero to zero in my eyes. I faked vomiting, hoping to make him feel guilty for what he'd done.

I always did love food, but gluttony was a problem that set in at an early age, and I was destined to be "husky." I met my first Americans and got a taste of their campfire fare, and I couldn't get enough! They called them hobo pies; buttered bread filled with jam and cooked in pie irons over the fire. God, were they good! I negotiated two for myself. I loved these treats so much that I looked for my friends from Indiana the following year and, despite being told that I was stupid, and that the odds of seeing them were slim to none, there they were. The hobo pies were back.

Well, that red bus was the start of our "on the road" spirit. It was sold for scrap years later for the same price as my dad had paid, and I heard it was painted green.

The guy who bought it was my dad's original neighbour, who once said, "John, you are a great neighbour. You're so easy to keep up with." The signs of minimalism were always there. After our first trip to Florida, despite my dad's love for the north, our lives changed forever. Years down the road, my parents sold everything, house, extra lot, and business, to travel for nearly

Carl Stars

thirty years in a fifth wheel trailer, with no fixed address, enjoying endless days of sunshine and sunsets.

7

You don't have to be rich to travel well.

— Eugene Fodor

My parents were certainly not rich, but it seemed we had endless vacations. When I was young, I didn't realize that most families of four don't drive thirty hours to the Florida Keys to cook outdoors and sleep by the ocean in the back of a four-door pickup tarped in orange. I have since grown into a "five-star hotel guy," but to get close to the real action of the ocean, this "rough" lifestyle made it happen, and still does to this day.

Travel changes and influences you. Turning thirteen after coming home from the first trip, I felt older in many ways. My music influences alone had launched me into an older crowd.

For my whole life, I would hang around with people ten years older than me.

My friend and neighbour once asked me to a Johnny Cash show. She and I had been friends for our entire childhood, but we had both entered a budding new phase in our lives. Although I remember the concert in its entirety, I was not prepared for the distraction that her breasts brought to the experience. It wasn't long afterward that she sought out the company of older boys, rather than mine; girls seem to mature so much quicker.

This first concert would lead to a lifetime of concerts. I picked up playing the guitar, though it remains my nemesis to this day. I don't play it well (never did), but it is an incredible form of therapy. As a kid, I played in a garage band called "Cranberry Sidewalk." We were christened by a hippie, high on mushrooms. I was kicked out of the band for being overweight, and I ended up playing Christmas music in a school play. I guess they thought they were going on tour!

One day, there was a knock on the door. A lady was given my name, and she offered my parents an ice cream franchise. I was convinced to sell ice cream at twenty percent commission. I was skeptical, but the only other job choice I had at the time was cutting grass, and I didn't want to continue doing that. My brother had excelled in the job, but I could barely get through the day—I hated physical labour.

The first few days I peddled the bike I endured a few beatings and more teasing than you could imagine. People taunted me with, "Dickie dee, dickie dum, stick your ice cream up your bum." The police were called to deal with the assault. The job caused me so much grief.

After a few days, I lay awake and realized I had made good money in Florida doing odd jobs and wondered, "Why is this job so difficult?" I realized that I was working hard, not smart, so I picked up schedules for swimming lessons, soccer games, and baseball games. My family would load up the bikes and I would hustle. I would sell lots of ice cream and not have to peddle. In a way, I contributed to the "Florida Fund." On top of driving a truck, my father also sold ice cream at the county fairs. I was teased so much, but when we went to the Florida Keys for our winter holiday, I would have the last laugh. My parents were capitalist hippies.

Sales were brisk! Even selling twenty-five cent items, I would leave one event with eighty to one hundred dollars, reload, and catch the end of another game. I would often net twenty to thirty dollars for a few hours work—easy work was right up my alley! One time I was nervous when a hippie character demanded ice cream and offered me marijuana in exchange. I was afraid to get beat up, so I took the joint and gave the hungover hippie an ice cream popsicle. Ever the entrepreneur, I sold the joint to a kid who was hanging out on the steps of the Bank of Nova Scotia.

I could have earned my way into a franchise and made "grown up" money as soon as I was sixteen. However, I made the classic wealth mistake that everyone makes: worrying about what someone thinks of you. I can assure you; many of the successful entrepreneurs I met in the Florida Keys had made it there at a young age because they did not conform to society's checklist of life.

While working on my ice cream bike, I made a treasured friend. Every day, she was at the park. I confess that I, along with every boy in town, had a crush on her. She was the daughter of a lawyer and I figured that she must be rich. Well, after weeks of friendship-building (okay, and the odd free ice cream), I was invited to her house for a visit.

When I got there, her father was stacking wood, and I decided to join in the labour in an attempt to impress him. After twenty minutes, soaked with sweat that was partly from the work, but mostly from nerves, I asked the man if his daughter was home. He replied, "No, she is in the States with her mother." I was so deeply embarrassed that I froze, then dropped the wood and ran home. The reason to stack wood was gone.

The one good thing from that summer was that I had saved, in a short amount of time, about $1000. This meant that I could start my first year of high school looking sharp! No more hand-me-down clothes; no more "husky" corduroy pants with stupid sideways stripes. I insisted on shopping for my own clothes, and purchased expensive golf shirts with alligators on them.

I started school looking and feeling good, as I had a little more money than my classmates. It was time to kick back and enjoy grade nine. For me, that's when my life really took off. Although my brother silently endured high school, I loved it.

8

There is a sunrise and a sunset every single day, and they're absolutely free. Don't miss so many of them.

— Jo Walton

In 1978, I could hear my parents talking in the kitchen. At this time, I still shared a room with my brother. It would be two more years before my grandfather would pass away and my brother would inherit his room upstairs. This was before the time of the "a child must have his own room" mentality. My parents, despite having very average wages, were extremely good at managing money. My mother could take a quarter and turn it into a dollar, making clothes and home-cooked meals. Nothing came out of a box, and a soup bone could bear an extra meal. Once, when we had a street-wide garage sale, my mother bought a shiny ashtray for fifty cents from a neighbour. She placed it by her handknit sweaters, and a lady came by minutes later and wanted to buy it. My mother initially told the lady that it was not for sale, but sensing an opportunity, she softened her position. Five dollars later, the ashtray was sold!

My parents were discussing pulling my brother and me out of school for a trip to Florida. My father's job was seasonal, and he had the winter off, so a mid-winter trip was desirable. However, my teacher didn't think it was a good idea and was recommending they not pull me out of school, even for two weeks. I was an average student, at best. Not only did I clearly have the problem of reversing my letters and numbers, my attention span was limited. When I was interested in something, my grades were good, but I wasn't interested in much at school. I had high marks in history, but my English mark was deplorable.

My parents arranged a meeting with Mr. Fewster, the public school principal. He wore thick, black glasses that made him look like a NASA scientist in a 1960s movie. He knew me well as I was sent to the office on several occasions, deserving the strap (he never strapped me, but he did strap my friends). Fortunately for our family, Mr. Fewster knew the value of travel, and felt that I would learn more on a vacation than in school. My parents would have the opportunity to homeschool before it became cool.

My lesson books were organized. I had text books on the basics: reading, writing, arithmetic, etc. My mom became my teacher and, despite her thick accent, her Norwegian/English mix would prove to be an asset. I would return to school a stronger student, much to my teachers' surprise and chagrin. I was near the top of the class at least for a while.

Packed and ready to go, we met up with Bob Leech, a fellow truck driver and Teamster who had somehow convinced my father to head south. He had a champagne-coloured Champion motor home and a swimming pool; I was convinced that he was rich. He sold the Florida idea to my dad and mom, saying the fishing was great.

The ride down was exciting! I saw billboards for the first time—advertisements for Stucky's and The Waffle House (where you could get a stack of pancakes with a massive amount of whip cream and fruit). It was my first time eating out in the States, and the portion sizes were epic! I loved the billboards and could not understand why we didn't have them in Canada.

In Florida, we passed by orange groves, pecan shops, and various tourist traps. The drive across "Alligator Alley" was the coolest. Gas seemed to be so cheap. Everything seemed cheap to me! We drove down in a brown, four-door pickup with orange tarps. We also had an old Woods canvas tent, and the cooktop my mom had salvaged from the red bus, which was now a distant memory.

Finally arriving in Homestead, Florida, we bought vegetables at a roadside stand, by chance near a prison. I saw prison workers and wondered if they made prisoners work in Canada. I didn't see it then, but years later I would see the Coral Castle, which was built by a Latvian. It is considered a mystery how this place was built. A tourist attraction some say hold the secret to the pyramids. The mystery of how one man could leverage huge pieces of coral was fascinating.

I cannot describe the smell that surrounds the bridges in the Keys; it hits you like a ton of bricks. It's the smell of the ocean, a salty, seaweed smell that some don't like. For me, when I think of it, it makes me think of home. The bridges were narrow and outdated; not meant to accommodate the modern recreational vehicles that now made their way south. It was not uncommon for large motorhomes and campers to lose a mirror navigating the bridges.

We finally arrived at mile marker thirty-three, the location of Big Pine Key Fishing Lodge. My life would never be the same.

I had managed to save eighty dollars, which was a lot for a twelve-year-old. I told my dad that I would make it stretch; spend only a little each day. He warned me that it doesn't work that way. I felt he was stupid.

We got to the camp and the office was buzzing. The camp owner was named Joan Gladwell; her nickname was "The White Tornado." She ran the camp and was the first independent woman business owner I would ever meet. She was an astounding woman; she brought so much energy to her camp and it was amazing to watch. I found myself staring at her as she ran the store.

The campground was full of colourful characters. The first character "Chop Chop" would walk through the door, grab a six pack of Budweiser, and sit down on the "Liar's Bench." This was an aptly-named bench, parked between the palm trees, where people sat to exchange their grossly exaggerated fish stories. I visited him daily and made his ears bleed with my excessive talking, which he seemed to tolerate—he just took it in stride.

Then there was a big Swedish guy named "Big John." He became my Florida grandpa as my grandpa was at home. He had owned a liquor store and told me about his life when he was young. I don't think he liked being such a big guy (which I could totally relate to). I have met so many wonderful people at this camp over my lifetime, and almost all of them had nicknames: Canada Bob, Billy Bob, Ropehead, One-legged George, One-eyed Chuck, Chicago Al, and Ms. Rustic, to name a few.

We spent endless days fishing and shelling in our boat. There was a guy in the camp that sold shells: rollers, whelks, or queen helmets. In those days, there was little regard for the environment and overfishing. The Florida Keys now have sanctuaries, and environmentally, they have made progress. You can't get local conch in Florida anymore; it's all imported from Jamaica.

I once ate raw conch with lime and tequila when I was seventeen years old and hanging out with a hotdog salesman from Kentucky, Shep, and One-legged George. Shep and George called me "Newfie," a nickname that didn't stick, but one that I didn't mind. There was something so special about waking up beside the ocean and blowing into a conch shell to wake the camp. I felt like a Viking.

The open camping environment attracted a lot of characters. The campground was a cross-section of society, and was perfect in many ways. It was an idyllic society, where everyone was accepted. The individuals who had opted out of their traditional "checklist" lives were happy just to be living a simple existence beside the water. There was even a "fitness guy" who spent hours obsessing over his body, clown nose on his face. He balanced on a log all day and tanned every inch of his body.

We had a natural saltwater pond; the water level fluctuated with the ocean tides. I swam in there for hours, despite the rumours that a large barracuda had made it his home. I'm pretty sure the rumour was just to scare me. Everything was brand new and exciting, and I spent most of my time outdoors. But when the weather was bad, I visited the rec hall. My introverted brother had no interest in joining me, and preferred to fish off of the bridges by himself in the rain. Kids much older than me would hang out in the rec hall, and they introduced me to music that would change my life. I heard "Lady Jane" by the Rolling Stones, "Mannish Boy" by Muddy Waters, and "Free Bird" by Lynyrd Skynyrd. I remember the college kids still crying a year after the plane crash that killed the band. I had discovered southern culture and southern rock and blues. That place shaped my life in significant ways, and my memories of socializing with the older kids are vivid ones. My musical tastes that were shaped there made me instantly cooler than my grade seven peers upon my return to Canada.

It was there that I met the Morgan boys. We would play this weird song "Cattle Call" by Eddie Arnold and shoot endless games of pool. These young guys were from Burlington, Ontario, and had parents like mine who valued travel. We all had the rare opportunity to grow up in the Keys, off and on, over the years. Years later, I met up with one of the Morgan Boys from the Keys for dinner, and I discovered that we both found occupations in people-based businesses. We agreed that our exposure to camp life had honed our abilities to talk to and be comfortable with older people, a valuable skill in itself.

In a small camper covered in lobster buoys lived a Hemingway type character named Roy. He had sold everything he owned to live a minimalist lifestyle on the edge of the ocean. I was not that great yet at living a minimalist lifestyle, and my money was running out. The ocean provided me a great deal of happiness, but so did money. I was getting nervous, as my parents had made it clear to me that they wouldn't be giving me any spending money. Their gift to me was this holiday, and the extras were my problem.

So, I found myself out of money. No money for ice cream, drinks, the pinball machine, the jukebox, or pool! Luckily, Monday night was bingo night. I snuck some quarters from my mom and turned them into fifteen dollars. I was alive for another day!

There were a lot of days when we had to stay off the water because it was far too windy for our small boat. But on the days when the weather was fine, I would get out fishing and we would catch lobster, and often go shrimping at night. Still, I was plagued by my lack of spending money, and I spent a lot of time wondering how I could balance my laziness with a good money chase (welcome to my life's obsession). What I came up with was this: I put up a sign on the camp's bulletin board that read, "ANYTHING FOR A BUCK, INCORPORATED" (I had heard that if you were incorporated you didn't need to pay tax). I couldn't fix things, but I was young and fit and could move things, and that was my edge.

My first job was to spray a man's boat with bleach, wait twenty minutes, and then scrub the bottom of the boat as it hung in a sling above the water. I was happy to do this job! In fact, I was so excited that I hadn't negotiated a price. How happy

I was to be handed forty dollars for less than an hour of work. I was instantly rich!

My second job was to tar the roof of an old camper. I used far more tar than was necessary (how could I know?), but I guaranteed the owner that his trailer was now "leak proof." I received fifteen dollars for this job.

My third job required muscle and discretion. I was asked to dump a washing machine in the mangroves out back. I rode along in the truck and helped carry the machine into the underbrush. I got ten dollars for breaking the law and holding my silence.

Next, I dug a hole for John Dunn, the camp notary and the same guy who had me tar his roof. The hole was for a telephone pole. I held onto the pole while he set it. He had forgiven me for using so much tar, and he paid me twenty bucks. As the camp notary, he would later marry my wife and me for twenty-five dollars, so he got some of his money back.

My piggy bank was filling up with all of this cash. The more money I had, the lazier my mindset became. I was hired to wash Chop Chop's car. It was a hot day, and I was not motivated to do a good job. I missed my friends at the rec hall. I washed the car and did a very poor job. Even as he handed me twenty dollars, I knew that I couldn't take that much. I gave him thirteen dollars back, as that's what I felt that the job I'd done was worth. Instead of going back to work and cleaning the car properly, I allowed myself to give a cut rate for a job poorly done. Maybe that's why I never got rich. It turns out that Chop Chop was a rich guy, masquerading as an impoverished soul, and that he had actually been pleased with the job I'd done. There's a good life lesson.

In all, I earned ninety-two dollars. It seemed that these old people had lots of money and didn't mind spending it! I was rich, and there was a round of ice cream in it for all of my friends. Still, my laziness had kicked in, and all I wanted to do for the rest of my holiday was to have fun in the ocean and hang out at the rec hall. Our stay was tenuous, as it was—my father was checking in regularly with his boss, Roger. Our family would huddle around the pay phone as dad chatted with Roger, asking if he was expected back at work yet. Fingers were crossed as we waited for that euphoric moment when Roger would tell dad to stay another week.

My homework was done, I had money in my pocket, I was in the best place in the world, and I was allowed to stay a bit longer. Life was grand!

9

Question: *What did the shark say to the clownfish?*

Answer: *You taste funny!*

The Florida Keys held an incredible draw for me. I was in grade seven when I first went down there and, had you asked me then, I would have told you that I would never again skip the opportunity to return. Still, I did opt out twice when I was in high school. It sounds rather entitled, I know, but I had other things going on at the time; incredibly fun times were not to be missed.

I spent four weeks one summer with this great girl, only to get dumped. It would be my first time enduring heartache! Her rich boyfriend returned from England and she went back to him.

He literally said, "Thanks for taking care of my girlfriend." That was rough.

While my parents were in Florida, I essentially had the house to myself. I hosted some great parties there, and alcohol consumption was a priority.

I always maintained the "checklist" life, even in high school, doing what I was supposed to do. Work, sports, party, fun—these things amounted to rounding out the best years of my life. I had taken an extra subject each semester, hoping to speed up my high school career. I felt a tremendous amount of pressure from my cousins (no, not from my parents) to raise the bar and aim high. My parents just wanted me to be happy, and advised me to "aim low, and you won't get disappointed." My cousins, however, were both successful, and there was no question for me that I should be the same. I should have listened to my parents then. Why does society not value the pursuit of happiness?

My cousin would pull up to our small town in a Cadillac, and it made me feel a little embarrassed for myself and my parents. I found his wealth intimidating. In those days, a man was judged by the car he drove, and you might have thought that my cousin had it made. Now, almost anyone can afford to lease a status car.

Still, at the same time, I was drawn to have what my parents had—the freedom to go to Florida and forget about the rat race. They were now able to spend even more time there, and were planning to stay for a full two and a half months. When I finished high school early, I could join them!

So the time had come where I pulled the plug on life (a habit that would be formed for life). I worked hard so I could do nothing. I wasn't even old enough to vote and I was already addicted to taking excessive time off. Screw "the people's master plan" and trade it for leisure time in the sun amongst the palms. I'm glad I have done this throughout my life. Life is pathetically short, and as I look at the photo of my grandfather now, I realize we all court death as the time clock runs out.

The trip down after high school was memorable. We went to a campground where the trees were hung with heavy moss—a Cyprus swamp. We paddled our canoes into the middle of a lake before spotting alligators sunning themselves on the shoreline. I'm not sure if we were stupid or fearless, but we did it. It was the most amazing place. Years later, the song "Seminole Wind" by John Anderson would remind me of this place.

Further down in Florida, my father had arranged an extensive trip through the Everglades. We launched our boat in the Everglade canals. Along the route were washrooms where you had to sign in so that there was a trail of evidence that you had made it from one point to another. It seems like a dream, but we slept in the seventeen-and-a-half-foot aluminum boat with a canvas top. It was not unusual for a snake or some animal to cross the canvas above our heads. Can you imagine waking up at two a.m. to unzip the canvas and step to the side of the boat to pee, only to have two red eyes staring at you—a huge 'gator, who happens to be floating beside your boat, and who is as startled by you as you are by it? It was an amazing adventure—two days and two nights (forty kilometres), after which we were dumped into the Gulf of Mexico. If you want to read a story about the Florida Everglades, I recommend *The Swamp* by Michael Grunwald.

After we left the glades, we were reunited with our vehicles, and we continued on to Big Pine Key. I do not consider myself an outdoorsman, but my love for Florida keeps me close to nature, and I will endure the no-see-ums and mosquitoes, uncomfortable sleeping arrangements, and rough living conditions just to be there. Although I prefer the Holiday Inn most of the time, I wouldn't take it over this tropical campground and a red solo cup.

This trip, I had more than enough money saved, and the next two and half months would have me suffering from "Keys' Disease." During the day, I adventured with my parents, but at night I partied.

We liked to fish in Looe Key, which is now a sanctuary. We were not sport fishers, but bottom fishing people. We caught our food fresh daily, cleaned it ourselves, and returned to camp just in time for happy hour. I can never fully capture in words just how beautiful the days were, no matter how hard I try. The sun made it look like shiny Olympic medals on the water; water that was clear as glass.

Generally, after we had caught enough food for the evening, we would cast our lures and try to catch a barracuda, just for fun. One time, I looked down and saw an eleven-foot hammerhead shark parallel to our boat. Its eyes rolled back as it was swimming. I held my breath, unable to speak. It was the closest that I had ever been to such a wonderful creation. I just watched as it swam by our boat, struck with awe as if it was a work of art. It was as if the most beautiful woman walked toward you out of nowhere—the world stopped.

We were still relatively new to the Keys and we had a lot to learn about the ocean and marine life. Jaws has done no justice to sharks, but let's face it, they do attack. Ultimately, if you choose to swim in the water, you should swim like you belong in the ocean—don't wear flashy jewellery, and obviously, do not go in the water with a cut. One time, I had gotten some distance away from the boat, and I heard my mother yell my name and the word "shark." I looked past the boat and, to my horror, I saw that a large shark was circling. I began to swim towards my father, who was between me and the boat. My father, who could touch the bottom, began to take a few steps toward me, hesitated, and then walked in the opposite direction. I think that he thought he had a better chance of getting me into the boat if he got there first. This was an unusually large shark—my guess was that it was a hammerhead. As I came closer, I found that I could touch the bottom, and I traded swimming for walking. I watched as my father, who had made it back to the boat without being attacked, picked up a half-eaten grunt fish and threw it as far as he could away from the boat, and away from me! The second that fish hit the water, the shark fin turned toward it, and was gone.

This is a great example of how we humans are the outsiders and we must respect the ocean and what is around us. Even though sharks are rarely interested in us, we really do need a healthy respect for the water.

Thirty years later I would return to the Keys (you always come back) and take a chartered diving boat to Looe Key. My wife and I went free diving while the rest of our group had tanks. The reef was beautiful—ecotourism was awesome, and on the rise.

This was a wonderful visit too—I saw so much marine life! I absolutely love snorkelling but do it only on occasion. (I could never take up diving, as I have a hole in my ear drum from a tropical ear infection I picked up at a swimming pool at a resort in Cuba.) I was snorkelling at the back of the boat and suddenly a once-in-a-lifetime movie scene happened. I was in a large school of yellowtail (nicknamed "flags" if they are over twelve inches long). They are beautiful to view and delicious to eat! I just stared at the fish swimming all around my head. I zoned out like a hippie on weed. It was the most peaceful and serene moment I had ever experienced. And then, just as suddenly as they came, they were gone. The water around me became murky and a feeling of concern came over me. Fish are chased by larger fish . . . was it a barracuda? A shark? I could hear yelling through my snorkel. I grabbed hold of the nearby ladder and frantically climbed into the boat. The entire crew and divers were on the other side and the boat was tilting quite a bit.

Well, what had happened was that my wife had gotten seasick and her vomit was forming a chum line. The fish had gone crazy and literally were eating the bounty as it hit the wake. The yellowtail had scored a smorgasbord! The dive instructor said that it happened just about every trip out. There is always one unfortunate person that gets sick.

10

A lie gets halfway around the world before the truth has a chance to get its pants on.

– Winston Churchill

When you are young, no matter how good you have it, you will ultimately screw it up. Turning fifteen, your brain is going nuts and being your own person is one of the hardest things to do. At fifteen, the odds of embracing your individuality are often slim to none; we are so desperate to conform. I was about to make a big mistake.

In a way, I was my own person and I had two shining examples of being "real": my parents. I had endured a few beatings hustling ice cream, and now that show was over. I let my first opportunity of many go by. Imagine, by age sixteen I could have easily been making $30,000 a year with a distribution network, but the teasing was unbearable.

I had a group of friends that could have been called "The Gang of Four." We went into the Foodland and stole *Playboy*s and chocolate bars, and three guys made it out without getting caught. I was the fourth. I walked nervously up and down the aisles, desperate to steal something, but not having the natural nerve for it. I grabbed the first thing that I could find—coloured cake sprinkles. The task was to steal "something" and I thought perhaps it would be safer to steal something unexpected. I thought that I was free and clear as I hastily bypassed the cashier and headed for the exit when a heavy hand landed on my shoulder.

Inches from my face, a man shouted, "You tell all your friends not to ever steal in my store again!" I was terrified; so shocked that I pissed on the floor. My brother's friend worked there, and cursed my name as he was told to get the mop. It wouldn't be long before the whole town found out that I had disgraced myself. I begged them not to tell my parents, even when I knew that someone would.

Of course, my friends were nowhere to be found. Life lesson: you end up in the trenches, alone.

By the time I got home, my mother and father had both heard about what I had done. My mother was sad, but my father's reaction was what tore me apart. He said, "Son, I'm disappointed in you." His words ripped through my heart. I was sent upstairs to my room while they decided my punishment.

I was grounded for two weeks. Worse than that, I was being sent back to the store to apologize to Mr. Spratt, the owner. I dragged my feet the next day, turning a short walk into what felt like an hour. I arrived at the store only to find out that he wasn't there. My father sent me back the next day, and the next for a whole week. I dreaded each trip there. I recall dragging my hand along the stone retaining wall, the same way I did when I was little and on my way to school.

Finally, on Saturday, he was there. I walked into the meat cutting room to talk to him. I told him that I was sorry, and he accepted my apology. He was stern and still obviously annoyed with me. On impulse, I asked him for a job.

Mr. Spratt was stunned. "You want me to hire you after you stole from me?" he asked, incredulously.

I replied, "Well, if you paid me, then I wouldn't have to steal."

Even I was taken aback by the audacity of what I'd just done. Still, Mr. Spratt held back a smile and said he would think about it. I went to the store daily after that, and by Wednesday I was hired.

The owner's wife, Kaye, reminded me of the woman who ran the Florida campground—full of energy! I learned so much from the family about business. Tom, the one who caught me stealing, was a deep thinker and taught me a lot about life. I learned about the tax man, who was eager to take more and more of your money as you put in more and more of your time. It didn't make sense to me that anyone should work so hard, put in so many hours of effort, only to lose their money to taxes. It still irks me to this moment, but now I'm older and I'm in the acceptance stage.

My life was a constant and predictable routine: work out in the morning and train with the basketball team, go to classes, go to football practice, go to work, complete any homework, and be in bed by eleven. Rinse and repeat. Do it until you burn out. Recover in Florida. Was this what life was all about? Was this what everyone did, minus the bonus of having the Florida Keys to retreat to? Would this be me for the rest of my days? This was surely the start of my struggles—chasing "granite countertops," but craving sunsets. The quest for happiness would dodge me, and it would become a thirty-year search and struggle for acceptance until I finally found peace and gratitude in my life.

11

Memory is fiction.

— Keith Richards

When I was in grade eight, I went to Caledonia High School for my brother's teacher interview. That was the first time I saw Peter. Shiny black boots, black cords, and a gold rope hanging out of his pocket. He was wearing a bright white shirt and those legendary tinted glasses. I didn't say anything to him, but he had tremendous energy and presence.

    The following year, on my first day in school, he rushed over to me, calling me "little Norm." Determined to make my own name, I declined the excitement of the meeting. He liked my brother Hans Norman. Norman had a trap line, fished the grand river, and knew everything about trees and birds. I was not a trapper John. Peter looked at me and said, "Oh, dear chubby child, it will take you a while to get into my world," and he left me in the cafeteria. I realized I was a little asshole with a chip on my shoulder. Entering his class for the first time, I saw a *Bob Dylan at Budokan* poster, and I knew this teacher was cool.

I was walking down the hall in my acid-washed jeans (that were way too tight) and my white high tops, desperate to fit in, and as this teacher walked by me, he said, "Think thin, chubby child. Think thin."

Now I was in grade ten and, having been forgiven for my terrible attitude, Peter started to appreciate my antics. He taught me about communism, which was enlightening as my father had escaped from a communist country. He got me to argue against communism with another student, who argued for it. He sat back and sucked on his lemon Halls, letting the children teach themselves. That's how he rolled and danced through life.

He was the first teacher to inform me about the local Native land claim. Our home was in Caledonia, which was beside Six Nations Reserve. It dawned on me that my house was in the claim. I shouted, "They can't take my house!" He looked at me and in a perfect Pierre Elliot Trudeau impersonation he said, "Just watch me, just watch me…" I had yet to learn about the FLQ crisis in Montreal.

In grade eleven, a close friend said, "Let's sneak out of class, you go first." I went behind the portable divider and fell out the window. My friend had tricked me and closed the window behind me. With no choice and nothing to do, I went to the door to return to class. Peter disgustedly said, "Leave the class, chubby child, and pick a new career. Go see Ms. Guidance and find your own path."

Our Montreal history trip was legendary. Our class partied like rock stars, and Peter joined in. The train conductor tried to slow the party down, but Peter exclaimed, "This is part of their education." The conductor said we could continue to have fun. The next morning, I ordered breakfast with a shot of brandy, and Peter complimented me, saying, "You are so European."

On the way up to Montreal, Peter spent an hour trying to get into my head. I could do more with my life, and I could achieve more. His heart sank when I told him I wanted to be a bartender. In his own way, he was the first of many mentors that tried to convince me to raise the bar—to reach my own potential.

Peter walked me through old Montreal and gave me an extensive lesson on the history of the buildings and Quebec history. I felt recognized and appreciated. I always did well in history, and he knew I loved the subject.

In my final year, Peter always had a diary on his desk with some reference notes. All the cool students were in it, but I never made the cut . . .

One night, by chance, my brother and I played pool with him at Granny's Hotel, and we had a fun night. I was on top of the world. The next morning I went into class to check the diary. The diary entry went as follows: "Boring night ho hum ran into the blues brothers at the hotel. Another day tomorrow.........." It wasn't what I expected, but I finally made the diary.

He had eccentric teaching methods. We once decapitated a chicken by the Grand River in memory of Marie Antoinette. Today, this would never be allowed. In that time, we could say things you couldn't say today, and a sense of humour was key...

I can only imagine how many students he affected in a positive way. In my view, Peter Hill could be compared to the famous teacher John Keating in *Dead Poets Society*. Yes, high school was memorable.

12

I was always the happiest in the Florida Keys

– Carl Stars

Cruising through the water in the Gulf, my dad would drive the boat and I would be on the bow, looking for lobster antennas. Like my Norwegian grandfather who worked on a whaling ship in Norway, and his father before him, I was the spotter. After sighting an antenna, my dad and I would jump in the water, outfitted in masks and snorkels. Generally, the water was no more than five feet deep. My dad would position his net behind the lobster and I would poke a stick at it from the front. The lobster would back away from me right into the waiting net. Easy as that, fresh lobster for lunch! I felt sorry for my friends back in Canada, struggling through the cold winter and their final semester of high school. I had it made!

Occasionally at night, we went back to the Spanish Harbor Bridge and, depending on the tides, we would drop nets and catch shrimp in the outgoing tide. My brother would fish from the side of the shoreline and catch baby bonnethead sharks and try to hook a tarpon. They are very difficult to land. We would partially fill our white pail and bring the shrimp back to the campsite. My mom would cook, and we would feed ourselves and our neighbours. Generous portions of Carlo Rossi would flow (big jugs of affordable red wine), and so would the conversation.

My parents had their circles of friends, while I had developed my own; a much more interesting group. One of my friends was a one-legged Vietnam veteran called "Vietnam George," or "One-legged George." He lost his leg and half of his stomach in a land mine explosion. I learned things about the history of the Vietnam War, and I was appalled to hear about how he was treated afterwards by some of his fellow Americans.

One night, George passed me a joint. I was about to inhale when I saw the silhouette of my father in the distance. He was always lurking in the shadows. Though I knew that his eyes were on me, he didn't embarrass me. I hung out with George, his buddy Shep, and another guy who walked around in a robe like one of the characters in M*A*S*H. These guys had drugs—lots of them. Pills, pot, and something in a clear pipe that might have been Opium . The weight was falling off me. We would get high, gaze at the moon, and talk about life. George would drink his Miller beer by the ocean, the beautiful night breeze blowing off the water. One-legged George was real; a solid guy that you would take into the trenches. I dropped by once and he was high and eating his dinner. He offered me some and I declined. He scrapped the food in the garbage and said something about southern hospitality. He would give you the shirt of his back.

George's girlfriend sometimes drove us to Dick's Bayside in her old Ford Pinto. I rode in the back with the famous gas tank. I had heard this car had gas tanks known for exploding. We played pool for cash and listened to live music. The singer was beautiful, with hair like Crystal Gayle. She closed every night with a tribute song just for me—the kid from Canada—"Moonlight Mile." It was beautiful and the band treated me like gold. Her husband could play guitar like nothing I had never seen.

The town had an urban myth and everyone claimed to know someone who had experienced it—we would always hear in the bar, "That guy got a square grouper." I was told "square groupers" were bales of weed found in the mangroves. You could sell one for $10,000. One thing I do remember in those days was a lot of people were flashing big money around in these clubs. One friend I hung out with for a bit claimed to have found one of these bales. Those were crazy times.

Still, nothing lasts forever and it was soon time to go home. That turned out to be a lucky thing, I think. I was drinking a lot of beer, seven and sevens, and chasing them with shots of Zambuca. I tried cocaine for the first time, snorting it off the dash of a blue '78 Ford pickup. The pile of coke was a small mountain. The amount of alcohol and drugs I was doing was excessive, but it didn't seem like it that at the time. I didn't know then that I was setting myself up for using alcohol to cope with the difficulty of living a "checklist life."

In our last week, my father's friend, Roy, told me that I would likely never be back to the Keys, and that I should treasure my memories of this one time. There was always this idea that the last trip would be *the last* trip. But Roy didn't know me well. He didn't understand the pull of the Keys on my psyche that would last me a lifetime. His generation worked for forty years, and then started living. I clearly had different ideas.

It made me very sad to hear, years later, that my friend One-legged George got knifed in the back of a taxicab in Costa Rica. I have no way of verifying it, but this seems to be the accepted version of the end of my good friend.

13

"All you need in this life is a tremendous sex drive and a great ego—brains don't mean a shit."

— Capt. Tony

I was back home now and high school was done; all my friends were off to University. Formal education never had a strong influence over my family. My parents are both smart, but never attended post-secondary institutions. My father was self-taught; he once read a full set of encyclopedias for something to do. I was already in the "cookie cutter" life trap—if you didn't go to University, you would be destined for failure.

I helped run a small restaurant known as The Caboose. A train caboose had been converted to a hamburger and fries joint.

The food was awesome and the french fries were incredible and addictive (they were dusted with Lowry's seasoning salt). I was way too serious for a young person—what you would call an "old soul." I partied with my friends, but I was focused on making money and trying to prove people wrong on the "loser" front. Happiness was not an option.

Despite my parents' objection, I enrolled in a restaurant management course at college. My high school history teacher, who knew that history was my true passion, was also disappointed. Everyone but me felt I could do more.

So, I was off to college, and sharing a basement apartment with my best friend. It was a huge change and I wasn't ready. After three weeks, I got the results of my first round of tests. My grades were high, and the mixology portion of the Food and Beverage course was exceptionally high (which was no surprise to me, as I had either made or drank the drinks before). And even though I was doing very well, I found myself suddenly bored beyond belief, and I didn't know what to do. I met a nice girl and drove to Hamilton to see her, with no plan. I spent time with her and ended up in a bowling alley with her in Hamilton. Her mother drove me home. I was a lost soul. I was used to being chauffeured around, and I really thought I knew everything.

At that point, I really wanted to study history, but I lacked commitment, and in some ways, I was spoiled. I moved in with my cousin in Mississauga and rented a room. Without a second thought, I went to the college and quit my restaurant management course the next day, before the deadline, and received a refund, which was mostly my own money, but my parents had contributed some.

My cousin's husband Chuck arranged for me to work at the Electrical Utilities Safety Association (EUSA) in Mississauga, spreading wood chips and sawdust into huge piles. I'm sure they had a backhoe planned, but they knew the work would be good for me. I started out slow, and then finally accepted my fate. Then suddenly, the rain came. It was my way out of this gig. I walked into Chuck's office dressed like the fisherman's friend guy, water dripping off me. I was cold and damp and miserable. "Chuck, it's raining," I exclaimed. He continued working at his desk for a minute; then he looked up in his pressed white shirt and said, "Thanks for the weather report."

I just stood there and didn't know what to do, so I went back out, and started working again, reluctantly. About twenty minutes later, he came out and took me home. I was a lost cause.

My parents were concerned and my mother stepped in. They took me to a boat show and we looked at boats—I was thinking about the Florida Keys. My mom took me to lunch and said, "Carl, why don't you just be what you're meant to be? A salesman. You should sell houses."

Well, I had zero confidence at the time, and rejected this idea. I decided to pick new role models; my cousin and her husband. I got a job in a hotel in Toronto and found myself working as a front desk clerk. I struggled with the job description, and quit two hotels in two months, before settling into a family-owned hotel called The Cara Inn.

Life was very different from the small town I had come from. After a few months, I noticed a couple with the same name each checking in with different partners. After a few more weeks, the staff realized that we had a couple who had each picked the same hotel to have an affair. The hotel had one call girl who worked there and she had figured it out. She told me that eventually everyone gets caught. The couple met in the lobby one day;

there were no fireworks, just a nod and an understanding that the marriage was over. They went their separate ways, and it was truly bizarre to see.

One time, a booking mistake resulted in the third floor being booked for airline flight stewardesses, and the fourth floor for a junior A hockey team. The rooms were destroyed! My God, was everybody fucking everybody?

I met a beautiful Italian girl and we spent some time together, but I had to end it because she was super religious and I was being recruited to her church. I ran for the hills—having been raised by atheists. We had a Lutheran background, but church was not in the cards for me! If I could describe one aspect of my parents, we would be more like an east coast family: Work hard, but Friday night to Sunday night, party! Drinking all weekend was the norm, and it was only years later I learned that not all families lived this way.

I found my way, after six months, working in an accounting office for a controller and doing the night audit; processing food and beverage sales. The experience was valuable. We would do the books on the night shift, midnight until eight in the morning, and we would have to balance out to the penny. One loner guy on our staff who was old and still lived with his mom loved alcohol. We would go into the Pancake House on the airport strip and get drunk as billy goats. We would sleep in the hotel studio rooms and then clean up and do audit accounting. My life was nothing but working and drinking and sleeping.

I was homesick and missed my hometown, but I felt that there was no going back. My father, against all advice, was convinced by my mom to allow me to move home, and let me rent the apartment above our house. I had around $3,500 saved up. I was out of work and had money, so of course that meant that I was off to the Keys again. This time, I got my own site. On this particular trip, I found myself drinking at Capt. Tony's.

At this time, the Keys were changing. Cruise ships were stopping in ports and what was formerly the "Wild West" was turning upscale; expensive shops and better clientele. In the old days, you could be drinking with gays, transgender people, sailors, and divorcees who were hiding out and skipping their alimony payments. It was a crazy time. A movie called *Cuba Crossing* does a really good job at showing what it was like inside the bar. I was even offered the chance to be an extra in this movie, but I had my own life to return to.

During this trip I finally got the chance to meet Tony. I was drunk and cocky and I was playing pool. The table had a lean to it, and I knew about it, as I had played on it before—I jumped a ball on the railing that went down the railing and dropped on the felt behind the stripe, and I sunk the eight ball. It was a fabulous shot, and Tony came over and shook my hand and said that in all his life, he had never seen a shot like that! I was feeling invincible, and I think that his coming over saved me from getting the crap kicked out of me.

He bought me a couple of beers and I was pumped that I was meeting the legend. I had two more large beers and stumbled out of Tony's and slept in the back of a van in a parking lot . I was glad to have had the opportunity to drink a couple of beers with Tony and I spent a lot of time there after that. In the early days, this bar is where I received my education.

Here's something I learned: The people that are often admired create a legend about themselves. Tony had done this with fishing, smuggling, and God knows what else. I recently read his book, *Life lessons of a Legend*. This is a must read. His crazy life was remarkable. Captain Tony was kind and was always compassionate. I wanted to be around someone who lived his life in such a big way. Still, my money was dwindling fast and I had to get home.

I was a college dropout; unemployed with no idea what to do. I wouldn't make it back to the Keys for three years, but it was time to get on with the show. I was so terribly unhappy doing what I was "supposed" to do. I wasn't figuring things out, either, and I felt that I had lived a lifetime already. I had combined drugs and alcohol, and chased sunsets in the Keys, so what else was there?

I visited Tony's again twenty-five years later and was happy to see that it hadn't changed at all. The town had, however, and was flooded with tourists, and the T-shirts were flying out the doors. I was in the bar, drinking, while my wife was shopping nearby, looking for Kino sandals, when Tony walked in and yelled, "Play some Bob Dylan!" Some tourists unfortunately ignored him; the bartender had a few words with him, and Tony left. Some people had no idea who Tony was, and what a legend he was! This was the last time I saw him. The legend, Anthony Tarracino, died in 2008 at the age of ninety-two. He had an amazing life and was a big player in Key West. He had even become mayor.

14

Life comes in big waves and small waves, rarely calm.

– an old Latvian Friend of mine

Skip ahead to after I dropped out of college. My so called "life education" was complete, and my parents tolerated my prolonged adolescence. I was paying an affordable rent, as my parents had hammered into me the idea of responsibility. And though I was working as a billing clerk in a run-down trucking terminal, I wasn't making much money. It was then that my father made his famous "twelve dollars per hour" speech.

My father referenced a work scenario: all truck drivers make twelve dollars per hour, but live radically different lives. My dad would scrimp and save, my mother made our clothes, and they lived frugally. If the furnace broke, my mother would reach into a sock or tin can for money that she had tucked away. My father worked odd jobs to supplement his earnings. Together, they worked at stretching their income and maximizing their savings. Inevitably, his work buddies ran out of money before every payday. They blamed the government for their shortcomings, but the truth is, they orchestrated their own unhappiness by being terrible money managers.

My father was savvy and gauged the economy by the number of construction cranes on the skyline. When there were only a few, he knew that hard times were coming.

I did not consciously follow my father into the trucking industry; it was the only job available to me at the time. For the next twelve years, I would endure setbacks, layoffs, and company bankruptcies due to deregulation. I started my career in a time of recession, where sayings like "let's try and survive to ninety-five" were words of hope. I moved around in the company: from dispatch to operations to sales.

I got to work by bus, making three transfers. At night, I had to hitchhike home. My transportation problem was mine to own, as my parents felt that I could move to be closer to work or manage my money better so that I could purchase a car. I chose the second option and bought a '77 Monte Carlo in the spring. It was red and floated on the road like a boat. Unfortunately, that car sat in the driveway for more than three months because my parents would not add it to their insurance, and I couldn't afford my own right away. Hard and cruel lessons!

It felt hard to be a grown up, and the life lessons were still coming. I discovered a beautiful thing called Visa—a shiny orange card that made the good times roll! The very day I opened my mail and got the card my best friend called me and invited me to Las Vegas. That card took me to Vegas, even when I couldn't afford it.

I loved to drink. It was not uncommon for me to drink a six pack at work on the evening shift in the trucking office. It was part of the work environment, something that you wouldn't see today, but those were different times. I visited my friends at University on the weekends, partied all weekend long, and then went back to work on Monday. I spent so much time on campus that one student wondered why he had never seen me in class. I juggled my youth and career with great success!

Working brought me closer to the "checklist life." Jimmy and Charlie were two guys that worked together at the same company for forty years, and strove for their "gold watch" rewards. I was terrified of this reality. I had a good life, didn't I? Jimmy warned me that the game was rigged. You pay off your car and just when you think you're getting somewhere, your car breaks down and you have to buy another one. You have one expense after another and it never ends.

Jimmy was a Korean war vet and he had amazing stories. He was very different from One-legged George though. Jimmy never talked about his time serving.

Charlie was a hot-tempered Italian who trained me. He would grab me by my mullet-type hair until I got it right. At the time, there was no HR department to complain to about having your feelings hurt. Truly, I feel indebted to these two fine gentlemen for what they taught me about work life.

Unfortunately, my partying was clouding my judgement. I was spending a lot of money on my lifestyle. I had entered into sales and was drinking quite a bit. It's hard to explain, but drinking was a big part of the job, even at the workplace. On my first business trip to Montreal, my sales manager fell into a plate glass window (which didn't break, thank goodness). After that, I was working on the road, selling in the Niagara Peninsula area. Free trade was coming, the economy was slow, and jobs were disappearing.

I could have gotten lost during this time in my life, but the one thing that kept me grounded was a Kinsmen Service Club for young men that I had joined. These guys became instant mentors. I learned about public speaking and how to manage projects. It was easier to listen to the lessons being taught there than to listen to my parents! Between this club and my hockey league, there was a lot of drinking going on. My life had become busy and exciting.

I looked the part of a successful salesman. While my friends were just finishing University, I was already cruising in a car with a Cantel cell phone making sales calls to General Motors; handsome and important in my white, pressed shirt and red paisley tie, or so I thought. I was on my way up, it seemed. On my way up, until I wasn't! My sales manager called me and told me that the company was closing. He handed me seven paycheques and advised me to deposit them before midnight. Luckily, I had secured a new job quickly, but had to wait a few weeks to start.

With everything gone in the snap of a finger, it seemed only logical that I would take myself down to the Florida Keys for a short break.

15

Guests, like fish, begin to smell after three days. –

Benjamin Franklin

(I argue that this quote originated with my Norwegian great-great-grandmother, who passed it down the line.)

Well, I started the new job; assigned with the task of starting a division from scratch. No employees, no customers signed on, and a limited budget. On top of that, I had moved into an apartment (which, I must admit now, I grew to hate). I desperately wanted to get a house and conform; maybe get a wife, too. Ironically, I live in this apartment now as I write this book, to be close to my aging parents, and it is the happiest I have ever been.

We put so much pressure on ourselves, but in some ways I had it easy. I landed this $40,000 a year job, which, by all accounts according to the job description, should be a daunting task. My rent was barely four hundred dollars a month and I had no other expenses, really.

I tried opening a second retirement account, this time with the intent to leave it alone! I was going to live like a responsible adult and grow up. This is what my life looked like: small town friends, weekend parties, home-brew beer, and a forever-young mentality. I had good friends and an infatuation with a sweetheart (that went nowhere). We were twenty-seven and forever young.

A friend who just lost his girlfriend and job temporarily moved in with me. The economy was still lagging. My friend was supposed to be there three days, but this turned into three months. We had some happy times, but for the most part, I felt that I had done my good deed and was ready for him to move on. Weekend partying had slipped into weekday partying, which showed no signs of slowing down. He finally moved out after I lost my mind.

I was terribly unhappy in my new role, but why I wasn't happier didn't make sense. I had a golf membership that allowed me unlimited golf after work. My division was rocketing up; turns out my employees followed me like sheep. I worked hard and provided value, and I knew I would make them a good living. They knew it too. But to my surprise, even with my break from the trucking industry, customers (and I mean major customers) followed me in droves. In eight months (four months earlier than projected) I had achieved my targets. Revenue and growth and an amazing twelve percent return in profits. I had the most profitable division in the company and the accountants started asking me questions.

Why was I sad? Well, I had no gratitude for what I had achieved. The problem is that I was arrogant and spoiled. My task came too easily, and rather than enjoying the fruits of my labour, I got bored. It just wasn't challenging. I admired my senior manager, but I never had the balls he had. Much to my surprise, I found out why he was so confident. He was a lottery winner. Another one of life's examples of why you should never judge a book by its cover.

The few female opportunities had died out and I found myself in a Legion on a Friday night. An older guy in front of me ordered beers. He was alone, and I thought to myself, I do not want to become this guy. There had to be something more. I wanted out of that apartment so bad.

I went to work on Monday, and I was talking to the top salesman—he always beat my numbers for volume (not profit). His words shocked me. He brought up the fact that when we worked at another firm, I could never beat him. He was number one; I was number two. He said, "You see, Carl, you're a nice guy and I'm an asshole. I deal with assholes. You don't. There are more assholes in this world than nice people." His words really affected me because I knew he was right. We all cherish those unconditionally nice people because there are so few.

I had been receiving calls from my former workmate and the offers kept coming. I was loyal, but bored, and I didn't know what to do. I had scraped up some cash but was floundering.

One day I took the call: a steel coil had been hanging off the edge of a trailer. Luckily, no one got hurt. At that time, there was a debate in the industry over safety issues. My suspicion was not verified, but I wanted an equipment review. The trailer conversions were not safe enough. There seemed to be a little pushback—not on ethics really, but no proof. It was the excuse I was looking for. I quit.

16

A problem is a chance for you to do your best.

— Duke Ellington

Of course, after quitting I went to the Florida Keys for a week during hurricane season.

I enjoyed the rain. Even bad weather under palm trees is better than good weather at home. It was the fall, but something was different. I couldn't get a job. Questioning the logic of taking a holiday I did not need, I had the stamina to drive twenty-eight hours to Florida on the weekend, spend a week, and return home.

Still, after returning, I could not get a job. My fellow Kinsmen members gave me odd jobs. I recall stringing conduit in a chicken barn where the vents were closed, and the glue made me higher than a kite.

I checked the newspaper, which had at one time published twelve pages of jobs, and found on the now-reduced single page, the following options: catch chickens, babysit, or work as a baker two hours every morning. December had rolled around and my parents were off to Florida. I knew I could not sponge another vacation, and I had no money. Between my service club and the hockey club where I was a trainer, the parties were endless. Yes, I had my parents' house, but I had to pay the taxes and utilities—I was learning the harsh realities about the real world. I was bitter. I was not happy about not furthering my education and living the cookie cutter life; I had no girlfriend and no job. Maybe I was a loser.

Why had I not saved more? I had to cash in my first stab at retirement savings—my AIC Advantage II Fund that I was convinced would make me rich had crashed in '87 on black Monday and the fund never seemed to bounce back when I needed it to. I understood long term investing but did not have the personality for it.

My brother came to the rescue. He had tolerated my parties and now secured me a general labourer job at forty dollars per day. It was the dead of winter and we worked in wide open vineyard fields, facing strong, cold winds and long days. I wore three pairs of socks in my boots. We clipped the dead grape vines for a German proprietor who manufactured Christmas wreaths and sold them to Walmart. It was a tough job, tougher still while hungover, and my brother carried me through those days.

In the first week, I bought a thermos, which rolled out of the truck with a crash. After the cost of replacing it and paying for gloves, I came home with twenty-eight dollars. I felt like a complete failure. I had developed the taste for the "good life," and equated my success with my bank balance. Every small cost created a big setback for me—a plumbing repair bail-out by a friend was something I had never dreamed would ever happen to me. It seemed like everything was conspiring against me.

I kept my humour, though, and bumped up the morale of the Cuban migrant workers. They hardly knew any English, and they would say, "Clip, clip." One day, I made a crucial mistake and cut a live vine. The German came up to me like a character from

Hogan's Heroes and said, "You must understand!! Zee one dead bush is lost contract!"

I snapped and said, "I don't have time to check for a pulse." The German had no choice but to laugh. His two blond sons, eight and ten, worked like robots and were already men by comparison to me. We spent so much time with the Cubans, we started speaking like them.

When I fell behind, my brother would keep going. He was good, and happy to work. Once, the German asked, "Vat is ze time?"

The Cubans replied, "Four thirty." We went back to the barn and were awarded beers and meatloaf sandwiches. When the German realized it was only two thirty, it felt like a small victory! I hated physical labour.

Finally, we had a mild day, and I found out that neither my brother nor the owner could work. By some miracle, I was in charge that day. I supervised the loading of the truck; the Cubans worked and I floated. I took the bundles of vines, washed them in a car wash, and loaded them into a barn loft. It actually went better than my usual days, and even the owner said my job could have been worse. There was an Italian in the other field, pruning, and he (we think) would drink wine. He would yell, "Que pasa," and I would yell back, and the workers would laugh.

One day, the Cubans quit. They had secured better, warmer jobs in a meat packing plant. I had made it through the winter, with loads of parties. Even the Cubans landed better jobs than me. I was a hockey trainer for the Caledonia Corvairs and during playoffs I had fallen on the star player, who was faking an injury so the team could rest. In front of the whole town, my hockey training days were over. The player was out for the game. The season was over and I had secured nothing for myself.

I intensified my search for jobs but found nothing. Though I had made repairs to my parents' house for some damage as a result of my parties, there were still things in need of repair, and no money to pay for them. I would have to come clean to my parents, something I dreaded.

Two days later the phone rang. It was my old boss. Somehow, I had made a name for myself in my trucking career, my dispatching, and my two sales jobs, and my reputation produced tremendous results!

I bumped into the German farmowner in the Food Land I had stolen from years before; I was all dressed up in my suit jacket and white shirt. He asked how I was doing, and I filled him in on my success. He said, "Carl, you were the worst worker I had, but I kept you around because you were funny and lifted the morale of the workers." I look back on my time as a labourer with some fondness. My brother and I still swap stories of the field occasionally, and it may just be one of the best times in my life.

Although the week in the Keys triggered some unnecessary financial hardship, I had made it down again and that fall vacation was worth it. Bad weather and all.

17

Thinking is the hardest work there is, which is probably the reason so few engage in it.

— Henry Ford

Every industry has a sweatshop; they pay you well, and you get a taste of what the owners have. Human instinct is to rise or aspire to this, thinking you will be happy. My father warned me that money doesn't solve money problems. I arrived at the yard, and I saw my old friend George, with whom I had worked before, off and on. We were in a small shed that had been converted to an office. We had been outfitted with lots of shiny equipment, and we were both excited and ready to go. I cannot fully describe the electricity in an environment like this. The best way is to compare it to

The Big Short, the stockbroker movie, or the series *Traders*, on the CBC. Incredibly high stress. The difference this time was the targets were set, and you could never meet them—the bar was that high. After the first week, I knew I was "in" and I wanted out.

The job wasn't what I had imagined. But I was lucky to have it, as I had been humbled. I was on call twenty-four hours a day, seven days a week; working seven a.m. to seven p.m. and often getting calls at midnight. I did not know there were two sevens in a day! I had scraped together some money and rented a room with Smurf wallpaper. On the first weekend, while discovering a new town, I dropped in at a pub. Everyone was so nice! I commented on what a friendly town this was and soon after, realized I was in a gay bar.

The famous blues bar down the street from my rented room, Pop the Gator, had closed. My landlord was smoking weed continually and it came up through the vents in the room. I slept deeply and woke up with a box of Cheerios tucked in my arms. I realized that I had made a mistake.

When I talked to my boss about how I was struggling to make connections in the city, he said, "Want a friend? Buy a dog." I didn't want a dog, so I made friends with my money. I had money, and lots of it. I bought a townhouse. Only later did I discover that a murder had been committed in the complex. Obviously, I hadn't yet acquired any of my real estate skills.

The company grew and the chemistry between me and my partner was unstoppable. We continued to grow our success. A year later, our phones were ringing with customers from Ireland, Toronto, California, and Japan. Things were out of control and the money poured in. The drivers were the highest paid in Ontario and we were all doing great. I leased an SUV and, unbeknownst to me, the only thing the SUV did was increase the number of bills I was responsible for. But the push was on for "that" life—I had the house, I had the car, and I was on the lookout for a wife.

The SUV was a nice sled with all the bells and whistles. I had come from a small town and suddenly I had expensive polo shirts, twenty-dollar cigars, a fancy SUV, and a ton of cockiness. I look back at the person I had become, and I was a certified asshole. I had become something out of character for me: a money chaser. The business of making money became addictive. I had used up some of my previous retirement fund money to purchase a house, and set about, once again, to save for retirement.

Carl Stars

The trucking business was similar to the towing business, in that it had its criminal elements. But you never really knew for sure. We had employees that belonged to bike gangs, and we moved a ton of freight—some of it for cash. I often received cash bonuses. The money moved through me like water. My mortgage was tiny and rather than paying it off with the roommates I took in, I opted to head to Toronto every weekend and light the town on fire. This was a seven-year run of unprecedented growth (and seven years of night life) and I had, along with the owner, built the company up to forty-six trucks. I was on call twenty-four hour a day. We permitted loads from California to Nova Scotia. I had developed a passion for the industry and the money that came with it. I would essentially never take holidays; I just kept working. But after two years of non-stop action, I cracked and did another weekend run to the Keys for a quick fix.

When I awoke the first morning at the Keys, I met my new neighbours—two young guys from Kentucky. I was instantly jealous of them as they were skinny, wore dreadlocks, and had chocolate Oreos for breakfast. That would send me to the fat farm.

We went to Key West and saw the legendary band Toots and the Maytals. I have, to this day, never seen a show with so much energy! After the show, the conservative side of me kicked in and I went back to mile marker thirty-three to crash. My young neighbours stayed, however, and partied for two days with the band. They claimed to have missed meeting Keith Richards by two hours. It is possible, as Toots and Keith hung out, but highly unlikely. I hooked up with these guys, drank moonshine, and woke up on a picnic table a day and a half later. My behaviour was epic enough to be mentioned in a self-published book: *LUV I SAM*. This is another book about life in the Florida Keys. I almost got kicked out of the fishing camp where I had grown up. I was saved only by the goodness of my last name and the skin of my teeth.

I drove home for two days, and, because I was travelling alone, the border guards searched my car for drugs. I was never stupid enough to try to bring something back, so I was safe. No sooner did I cross back into Canada than the phone began to ring. My holiday was over and it was time to go back to moving loads.

I had worked for four years with this company, and knew in my heart that I was in the wrong line of business. The problem was that I was good at it. My silver tongue helped with sales. I liked half the job, but something was still missing. Why had I not pursued my true passion? To try to fill the hole, I registered at McMaster University for six credit courses. Two nights a week in the evenings I studied European history, starting with the Renaissance. I had accumulated so much knowledge from my own self education that I sometimes (discreetly) corrected the teacher. I enjoyed my courses, and was at a crossroads: study or work? The CEO of the company walked into the office one day and spotted a textbook on my desk. He asked what I was studying, and I replied, "History."

He smiled at me and said, "You make your own history. You will learn that one day." He dropped that bomb on me and walked out.

In my fifth year with the company, my boss and his partner got divorced and he had nowhere to go for Christmas. I brought him to Florida for a week for another run to the Keys. I stayed for two weeks and was able to reflect on just how miserable I was. It seemed like I wasn't the only miserable person in the company. The source of our misery, it seemed to me, was our collective greed.

What destroys companies? GREED. We had had a good thing going, but now all three partners were going through messy divorces. In addition to that drama, my immediate boss and a co-worker had both been star-struck by younger women, and this led to further distractions.

In a pattern that I'd seen before, there was a land purchase, followed by a decline in the economy, and the eventual downfall of the company. We were heading this way and it was unstoppable. We should have been excited to operate in our newly acquired space, but the excitement was gone. I rented out my townhouse, which proved to be an endless headache, and moved to the Burlington area. I began dating, but I was hopelessly addicted to my job and still put most of my energy toward work. The stress of it was taking its toll. I chose to ignore the signs my body was giving me.

How many people have died for what they believe to be "success"? I had once again become the burned-out tow truck dispatcher I had met in the Keys when I was young. I still had not learned. I came home from one shift and my left side collapsed. I slept till the next day at noon. The doctor said, "If you don't change your life, why come for an appointment?" I was a mess, but I had money.

And still, I partied on. I spent the weekend in Syracuse, New York with my closest friend. We enjoyed unlimited drinks in a bar in what was one of the most bizarre experiences of my life. The bartender would serve us our free drinks with some verbal abuse: "Here's your drink, asshole." She passed along her abuse and our drinks to us with an obligatory, "It's on the house." She thought we were off duty cops.

I met a brunette and the conversation turned to writing. She was amazing! I shared with her my dream to write a book about a man's struggle for happiness. The book was one that I kept largely in my head; it was titled *Man in the Basement*. She could relate, and we chatted about the search for happiness and whether it was elusive or attainable. Even then, I didn't have the answers that I feel I have now. I was too scared to make any big moves toward happiness; I only knew that I wanted to be happy.

By this time, I was mature enough to know that I was in a different place from most of my friends. I was having some one-night stands, while most of my friends were already married. I drank a lot of alcohol but didn't consider myself an alcoholic. I didn't NEED alcohol, it just fit perfectly into my lifestyle.

I was in Ellicottville, New York for New Year's Eve. I was never a fan of this night and all the hype surrounding it. Still, I brought my credit card along for another pounding and a good time.

I slipped out of the room just before all the slobbering began, and stepped out onto a metal staircase, which was treacherously wet and slippery. I fell down the whole thing and landed, unhurt, in a puddle at the bottom. I found this so hilarious that I just sat there laughing. Just then, the door swung open and a beautiful girl stepped onto the landing before I could warn her. She fell, too. There we sat, two strangers at the bottom of the stairs in a cold, parking lot puddle, laughing uncontrollably. We could hear the countdown from outside and celebrated midnight with a quick kiss. I knew somehow that things were going to be okay.

18

Summer will end soon enough. Childhood as well.

– George. R. R. Martin

The intense work continued, and I settled in. I knew things would come to an end; they just had to. I cannot explain the level of pressure on us to reach our revenue targets. We came off a good a year, as we had a slight rebound, and the bonuses were now going to the owners. The realization that I was making them a ton of money hit me hard, even though I was very well paid.

Socially, I had hit a ceiling. I had become the "older guy" in my crowd, and I found my friends were getting younger.

Our company hired a new accountant who would become a good friend. He was destined for greatness and with his high-level education credentials, we wouldn't keep him long (he eventually became the vice president of several major companies in the United States). We learned from each other—my experience and his positive energy benefitted us both.

I went white water rafting with his group—a *90210* crowd of young, entitled achievers—and I was the add on. I ended up in the "geek raft." Yep, misfit island was on this raft. We hit the first set of rapids. As soon as I saw the waves, I knew we were doomed. We lost some of our crew almost immediately.

By the second set, there were only two of us left and the wave hit. I found myself airborne, the helmet ripped off my head. The raft had a wooden bench, and I was hit hard. I was knocked out and under water for a brief second. When I came to, I swam in one direction like the safety person taught us, but despite my best efforts, I found myself going in circles. I was getting tired and experiencing what we had read about: the resignation and overwhelming desire to give up. I took in water and recall the feeling of it coming in. I leaned back and was going to sleep. Drowning is truly peaceful. As my head tilted back, I could hear a small hum. It was a boat motor. A large tube was thrown around me and I felt myself being pulled toward the boat. I was coughing, but I would live another day. The two lifeguards (who were *Baywatch* look-alikes) lifted me into the boat. I landed on the guy's foot, and we could hear a snap. "You fat fuck!" He was out for the summer with a broken foot. A hero's welcome greeted me on the shoreline as my new friends chanted my name. My near drowning had cemented my popularity, and I soared to the top of the group.

The next day was slow, and we took it easy; a much-needed recovery day. On the third day, we arrived at a bungee jumping base camp. Everyone had registered the night before, but on the actual day, everyone backed out except me. Fueled by four Budweisers and a huge ego, I proceeded to climb the tower. I had heard the tower was eighty feet high, but the pamphlet confirmed that it was actually 120. The climb itself was more dangerous than the jump as there were limited safety lines and the industry was not regulated at that time.

I remember standing on the platform and the instructor saying, "When you hit the water, close your eyes. If you want an extra jump, lean back and the bungee will bring you halfway up." Because of my sheer weight, I followed the instructions to a *T* and leaned back. On impact, the bungy snapped back and I was once again at platform height. I scored two jumps, then a third at about half the distance. I walked on air for weeks after this incredible thrill.

On the last night, I sat around the fire beside a beautiful Indian girl. I was doing well but struggled to remember her name because of my drink. I was asked by her to get a log for the fire. I lost my balance and the log landed hard on this poor girl's foot. I had successfully broken two feet in one weekend!

After the weekend away, it was back to my work routine. The craziness had become normal and, much to my dismay, I came to the realization that I had chosen an industry that was directly linked to the economy. People do not understand how critical transportation is and how it's an indicator of things to come. I was exhausted; always trying to hit those targets.

But another long weekend came and I was off to Bobcaygeon for an annual house boat trip. The year before, I had fallen off the lock's cliff into the water. My best friend and I then picked up two girls to come back to our rented boat. I hit the water miraculously without a scratch, but it was enough to turn off the girls, who quickly left. That night we drank beer and smoked weed. Someone dropped a live rock bass onto the kitchen table and we howled with laughter as it flopped around. When you party, everything is funny.

This year's trip was going to be more normal, I thought, as we were all older and more secure. Well, so I thought. We discovered gin and vodka martinis at the Locke 32 pub. We drank all night, with our boat parked in the lock. The owner flipped us for the bar bill and he lost! We left with no bar tab and free T-shirts. My friend and I went to another bar where we dove on couches. People were enjoying the craziness of it all. But I knew I had enough, and that it was time to go back to the boat to sleep. I actually showed signs of common sense. I wandered back to the boat, then realized that I didn't have the key, so I laid down on a nearby bench and dozed off. I was awakened by the police, who were responding to a call about a violent crime in the area. I explained my situation, but they were not at all motivated to verify my story, and I spent the rest of the night's sleeping in the Lindsay jail.

I was fingerprinted but released in the morning with no charges. As I was walking back to the boat, I passed a house where two guys were drinking on the porch. They asked what had happened, and I, embarrassed, told them the story. They were sympathetic and told me not to worry about it. You just had a wipeout. They handed me a beer, which I choked down in the back of their car as they drove me back to the marina. When we got there, the boat was gone.

No one had cell phones in those days. I saw another houseboat docked nearby and asked the girl who was tying off the line if she had seen my friends depart. She said that they had left twenty minutes ago and were probably headed to Fenelon Falls. Desperate, I told her what had happened and asked if she would take me there. After a quick discussion with her houseboat mates, she said I could come aboard. I volunteered to drive the boat and she joined her friends sunbathing on the roof.

I was clipping along when a girl came down in a white bikini and a halter top. She asked me my name and offered me a beer. She said, "I will call you Captain Carl!" and placed a Captain's hat on my head. The next girl came down and I was awarded with an egg salad sandwich and another beer. The second beer went down so well, and amazingly, I was back to feeling eighty percent. The girls yelled down to stop the boat, as they wanted to go swimming. Seven girls and I spent the afternoon swimming and playing volleyball. What a great day!

I pulled up alongside the friends who had abandoned me; a boat full of girls doing a twisted version of the can-can to ZZ Top's "She's got legs." I opened the window, and yelled, "All aboard!" (the famous intro to the Ozzy Osbourne song). I had gone from zero to hero again!

One of the guys "got lucky" in a friend's bed and wrecked the sheets. The next morning, we had to dive and retrieve his clothes, as his suitcase was thrown in the water as a retaliation.

It was a wild time, but this adventure was over. I'm left with this lingering memory—whenever I hear the song "Bobcaygeon" by the Tragically Hip, I think of myself leaving jail.

The next long weekend came in September, and I was off again to Wasaga beach. I had newly discovered the philosophy of Ayn Rand and individualism, which would contribute to part of my philosophy of life. As it was, I was only halfway into my intellectual journey as I had yet to read *The Grapes of Wrath*.

The owner of the resort hotel had discovered this book in the early '60s and we discussed it at length. It was great to be meeting amazing and interesting people. All kinds were mixed together and there was a myriad of people by the outdoor firepit. I met a great girl that weekend. We made love on the beach, and the next day her boyfriend turned up. It seemed to be a thing with me—the girls I slept with would, the next day, disclose the fact that there was a boyfriend or a husband in their lives. I have come to learn that, contrary to popular belief, women cheat way more often than men.

Though the weekend was fun, with the sparkling water and the beautiful days, it was time to go home. I was tired of the nonsense. I realized that it was time to make some changes. I drove the many hours home, discovered that I had my friend's car keys in the console of my car, and had to drive all the way back up north. The perfect end to the perfect weekend had turned into a nightmare of highway driving. I finally laid my head down at two-thirty in the morning. Still, it had been the right thing to do. I learned that you will always be judged by your actions. I had become known for, and continue to be valued for, having integrity.

Despite the short night, I was back in the office at seven a.m. When my boss asked how my weekend was, I replied, "Quiet." I put my head down and started moving trucks. In eight days, I would meet my future wife and my life would bring the change that I was ready for.

19

Marriage is something you should only do once.

– Carl Stars

I met this girl at a party and she seemed bored to a degree. Definitely an introvert so we were obviously a mismatch. After a typical new romance, whirlwind for sure, it was time to get married and conform to the master plan set for all.

   I recall being over-the-top happy at my stag in Toronto. I was thirty-two and she was soon to be twenty-four. I was happy and with my friends. I went to the bar and ordered shots. There was a guy who looked like an actor. His black hair was over his brows, he was sweating and mumbling alcoholic phrases. These are the smart people, and often anyone who has spent enough time in the bar knows this.

He looked at me, and said—out of the blue—"do you know why you are happy?" He replied before I could answer, "You are legitimate now, in society's eyes. Truth is, married people get more invites. People know when you're single, there are certain events you just won't get invited to. You are happy because you're legitimate, but it might not last." That said, I wasn't going to listen, and we were off to the Florida Keys.

I was hoping my wife-to-be would love the Keys. I had spent my whole life there. Much to my surprise, my perfect road-trip partner loved the Florida Keys and the fishing lodge—maybe more than I did. We actually made plans and major financial decisions in our marriage based the Florida Keys. If we do this, then we can't go to Florida? This ruled our decision-making process for fourteen years.

A typical young couple with no money, my wife-to-be purchased a dress for twenty-nine dollars, accompanied by a fourteen dollar flower bouquet purchased at Publix, and sandals for seven dollars.

Sunsets and Granite Counter Tops

The day before the wedding, we made a trip to the Key West courthouse to get our license. My dad drove us in his old Ford truck, which he still makes payments on after twenty years, according to him. That's his humour. My wife asked the clerk about the pink room and she was informed that's where people get married. We were tempted to do it right then and there, but our plans had been set.

In unique Florida Keys style, we had pictures taken by the ocean, right at the campground of the Big Pine Key Fishing Lodge. We actually got married by a buttonwood tree quite close to a fish cleaning table so the ceremony could be more private.

We were honoured to have Don and Maureen Baldwin with us; friends of our parents. Don read the ceremony and Maureen took the pictures. Our camp notary was John Dunn, the gentlemen I had worked for in the camp as a child. He was wearing a T-shirt with Bart Simpson on it the day before, but for the wedding day he actually had a more current shirt on—it had a sailboat on it. He was a typical Keys resident, laid back and happy.

During the ceremony, a very excited Dave Griffith showed up, and he couldn't wait to show his catch of the day (even though I thought I had the catch of the day). He plopped his cooler in front of my wife-to-be and me.

I said, "Dave, we were actually getting married here." He replied, excited and happy, that he thought we were rehearsing for one of the camp plays that are held at night for the campground residents.

So the wedding stopped as we held his daily catch and had photos taken. Not many wedding photos have pictures of the bride and groom holding fish. Typical Florida Keys.

Our dinner was at a roadside restaurant called KD's, with ample draft beer and chicken wings for all. My wife's friends had a little too much to drink and were forced to spend the night in my father's fifth wheel trailer. The next morning over breakfast my father asked our guests, "How was the first night with trailer trash?"

The campground, which provides a wonderful family atmosphere, threw a party in our honour. My dad contributed the rum, and Joan, the owner, served piña coladas.

I was now married to a partner who would continue the Florida Keys tradition. She wanted to chase sunsets and granite countertops. I wanted to chase only the sunsets. We were very different people.

20

When women go wrong, men go right after them.

– Mae West

We were living in a newly rented loft, and I was riding the wave of happiness—we had a trip to Florida and we had some money in the bank. As much as I thought I knew everything about self-employment, I didn't realize that making money is far easier than managing it.

We were a young couple, newly married and with very different philosophies about money. Although it was still very early in the marriage, at times I felt a real disconnect from my wife. We shared a love of the Keys and we travelled well together. In that sense, and in those circumstances, when every day was an adventure, we were well-suited. But in our everyday lives, with a nine-to-five existence, life was difficult. I was committed to make it work, though, as we had mutual dreams.

On August 14, there was a major blackout in Ontario and parts of the United States. I had confirmation that my wife was stranded in Toronto. I received a knock on our door; it was our neighbour, a gorgeous professional dancer. Even my spouse commented on her natural beauty.

"Is your wife coming home?" she asked. I told her that she wasn't, and we stood at the door chatting. Earlier in the day I had mentioned that it was my birthday. There she stood, in tight shorts and a super tight T-shirt and I wondered how she had not yet been discovered by Hollywood. She suggested that we have a drink and celebrate my birthday together. I knew what she was offering, and though it was difficult, I said, "No." I felt that a pilot light would last longer than these sparks.

A day and a half later, I was able to deliver gas to my wife and we drove home. I told her about my experience and she thanked me for being a good husband, punched me in the arm, and said, "You do realize you will never get a chance like this again unless you pay for it?" To me, my wife was the most beautiful woman. The girl next door later moved to Japan to take care of rich executives.

I was preparing to go on a trip to New Orleans to celebrate with a friend who was getting married. It was to be my second trip to New Orleans, and I was hoping to have a similar experience as before, with excessive amounts of everything Cajun; music, food, and spirit.

I was on the treadmill at home, desperately trying to get into shape, when I got an overwhelming feeling of dread. This was the first of several times that I had a premonition. I've sometimes had this feeling; saying goodbye and thinking, "I will never see this person again." I had headphones on and a Van Morrison refrain played in my head: "Baby, please don't go."Its actually written by muddy Waters I broke out in a sweat. It wasn't from the exercise—I just had a deep and creepy feeling.

I was in a bar on Bourbon Street when I heard Bill Wharton and the Ingredients. He was an incredible slide player. Many of his songs were fun and Florida-related. He wore a chef's uniform and had a large pot on a burner on stage where he cooked gumbo. He is known as the "Sauce Boss" because he feeds his audience gumbo after the show when they are good and drunk.

He donates a lot' to foodbanks and local communities. I met him a blues festival in Buffalo—he is a really nice guy.

Our crew was having endless fun together, and I let my guard down by allowing the wanderer in me to take over. I turned off Bourbon Street on my way back to the hotel when suddenly, wham! A bottle was smashed over my head. Three guys jumped me. I swung wildly and fell off a small median, landing in front of an orange cab and skinning my knees. I felt an anger rush into me that I didn't know I had, but this was a moment of survival. Back on my feet, I stumbled through the crowd, desperate to make my way back to Bourbon Street. I was sure that I would be just another casualty in a major city if I couldn't get out of there. I was loud and drunk and alone, sure, and these things had put a target on my back.

I was beaten so badly that I ended up in a hospital. I suffered cracked ribs, a small slice in my ear, and a concussion. I couldn't believe the luxury in that hospital! When I asked the doctor about it, he told me that because I had good insurance coverage I was brought to the private facility rather than the public hospital, where less fortunate people were lined up around the block to receive care. When I got back to the hotel, I called my wife and broke down, begging to come home.

I flew home and suffered from post-concussion syndrome (before it was a thing). I vomited for three days, and it was a slow recovery afterward. Still, after the recovery, I had another excellent "salesman story" in my pocket.

I'm sure some of my readers will feel skeptical about my uneasy feelings and the way things transpired, but the feelings were so strong—I should have listened to my gut.

When I got home, my trucking career was starting to collapse. My wife said, "It's okay to quit; why don't you sell real estate?" Just as my mother advised years earlier. I got my license, and I warned her it would be hard. I was humbled because real estate is a finesse business—selling was different here. I had run out of money, and with regret, was delivering newspapers in the morning. We actually had trouble paying rent. Every day, agents would come and go as I hopelessly stared at the phone waiting for it to ring. "It's ok, you will do well with your smile and personality." I learned that misery loves company. Then one day a veteran agent came by and I said, "I can't take it anymore."

She showed me her rebuilt Honda Accord, freshly painted. She then told me in simple terms, "Real estate can make you a good living, however, you must focus on net profit, not gross sales." In other words, get off your ass and work. She handed me a Mike Ferry training course, "How to Jump Start Your Production in Twenty Days," or something like that. She said to do everything on these cassettes, and if I don't sell a house in three months, quit!

I did it, out of desperation. I was fighting panic attacks, a new symptom I had never had before. By December a miracle of my hard work happened—I sold six properties in eight days. With the payroll system that was in place I had sixteen thousand dollars total.

My wife came home and said, "What do we do now?"

I said, "We're going to Florida," and off we went.

Real estate agents cannot manage money, and that's why so many fail. I have lasted twenty years in the business, and I really do owe it to that lady I met in the parking lot. I just wish I could remember her name.

When I returned, all those agents no longer talked to me. I had learned that, as soon as you do well, the judgement comes.

Many stories come from a rewarding career, and I could literally write a book about my clients; like the client who flipped a coin on whether to buy a house or not. He once said that all major decisions really come down to a coin toss.

My favourite real estate story is about a lottery winner who bought a reasonably priced home. They had been saving for a house, and the husband wanted to buy a lottery ticket, and the wife said, "No, lottery tickets are a waste of money." A fight erupted, but he bought the ticket anyway, it put the wedding in jeopardy for a few hours. The next morning, they had won the lottery.

The husband-to-be accused me of never talking to him. I had to let him down gently; I told him that his wife was the decision-maker. I said, "When you hear her squeal about a feature in the home, that's where you will be living." In the negotiation, I said to the home seller that I could not take the counteroffer to my clients, and he cracked and dropped the price. The real reason I could not take the offer back is that there was skunk on the front porch. After the skunk cleared, I did full disclosure, and the buyer and seller met in the middle. They live there to this day.

Fast forward to a few years later. My wife and I had managed to save for a home. It was a small bungalow in University Gardens, and, for me, it was like going back in time. How did we pick the house? In the same way that a customer of mine had (and I made fun of him for it)—the wife wanted it. KARMA! She wanted it NOW. And yes, she got it.

Summer was a series of barbeques and parties. We even had enough money to make it to the Florida Keys every Christmas. The streets where we lived were wide and everyone had a dog. My wife had picked the best neighborhood around. On the day we moved in, I smoked a joint, and said, "Well, here we are. Twenty-five years to go and it's ours." I was living the checklist life now! It wasn't that easy, being a bachelor at heart, and settling down to this lifestyle, even though I did love the place and my life.

But subdivision life gets boring. I was drinking less and doing everyday homeowner things, like going to the nursery and purchasing plants. I had a new Napoleon BBQ—it had to be the best one, as I had a huge ego—and life was good, but still I felt unrest. I poured all of my money into getting out of debt. All of my energy was spent scrounging for more money so that we could go to the Florida Keys, where I caught up with old friends and made new ones.

I should have invested more energy into building a better partnership with my wife. We learn as we grow . . .

21

It would be nice if they didn't make me get up at 5 am for a 12-hour day. My caravan is never big enough to lie down. There is no little doze. You are knackered by the time you get home. Knackered.

— Diana Rigg

The most valuable life lesson I have learned is that money doesn't solve money problems. I had doubled down on my efforts: trucking income, consulting income, real estate income, property management income. Yet there were times I wasn't working that hard. Mental exhaustion was the big thing—trying to maintain the show.

We spent a lot of money on maintaining our lifestyle; endless dinners at the Keg, breakfasts out, shopping trips to Grove City. We averaged four weeks of holiday at a minimum, including a couple of trips to a timeshare in North Carolina. www.rumblingbald.com is another gem. Our combined income was good, and our shared motto was "work hard, play hard." The only problem is you get tired. My wife was working sixty hours a week, plus an extensive commute, to pay for our house taxes and mortgage. We were "DINKs"—Double Income No Kids. We were selfish, but we wanted the same thing: the Florida Keys.

We were looking forward to making it to the Keys, and this time we were on the direct oceanfront site. The wind from the ocean eliminated the bugs, and the sunrise and sunsets were worth every penny. We had only chipped out about ten days for this holiday. Our dog, as always, was placed in the doggie daycare, though I hated doing this. I was never one for pets, but Banjo was the best dog ever. I was converted from a cat person to a dog person by him, and he was both my joy, and the bane of my existence when I was working from home.

We arrived—We had made it back to the Keys! I was looking forward to the best week ever. Money and minimum payments were maintaining the shit show and we were relatively happy. The next day at two a.m., disaster struck. I had a temperature of 103° F. I was off to the hospital, and I was a mess. For the sixth time in my life, I was diagnosed with pneumonia. I attribute the pneumonia to my terrible lifestyle. I have done a lot of research on the immune system since then, and have made significant changes to my lifestyle that have paid off (look into it!). I am happy to report that I haven't had pneumonia since that time, fifteen years ago.

We drove all this way, twenty-eight hours in all, and all I was only able to enjoy a short boat ride before becoming sick. After leaving the hospital, I pulled out my credit card and took a motel. I slept for a week while my spouse sunned herself by the pool. As if this wasn't bad enough, a hurricane was on its way and we had to leave the Keys in a hurry. It was a "bug out," like a MASH unit.

My wife gets the credit for hammering home for sixteen hours straight. This woman could drive like a robot. We made it all the way to Statesville, NC, with me sleeping the whole way. Five days of sleeping, and I still needed more! We stayed in a motel overnight and hit the road early, as a winter storm was brewing.

It was at this point that our commute turned into a nightmare. I was actually feeling well enough to take over the driving at the New York line. The road signs were flashing messages about inclement weather road closures, and we were snowed in.

We came across a van (still running) in a ditch. A family from a local Native reserve was stuck, and they didn't have winter jackets or water. I always keep calm in these situations. Two other vehicles showed up: a Jeep and an SUV. I asked the family to split up, but the parents were reluctant. I arrogantly said, "They make minivans all day long. We have to get you to safety." The family was split, even though the other drivers were hesitant to take on the responsibility.

The guy in the Kentucky Jeep wouldn't lead the pack. He said, "You're from Canada, you should lead." Americans think we are in winter ten months a year—I swear! The other guy, from Syracuse, was holding back tears. So I took the lead in a two-wheel drive Ford Escape, going five kilometres per hour. We used marked signs on the road to stay on the road, and it was hell. It was very scary. My spouse, out of exhaustion, broke down and cried, as the drive took tremendous energy and focus. As we got closer to Fredonia, NY, it became a little lighter, and I sped up to fifteen or twenty kilometres per hour. In the rear-view mirror, I could see that we had developed a caravan of about sixteen vehicles. We made it to the tollbooth and found that the operators, unbelievably, were still collecting! I guess taxes and death are guaranteed. The toll booth guy told us that it would be impossible to find a hotel room and directed us to the nearest Red Cross shelter. We spent the night in a gymnasium with two hundred snoring, coughing, and farting strangers at Fredonia High School. I imagined what my father went through, escaping the Soviets and living as a refugee in Sweden.

I looked across at my wife and she was smiling. The journey is part of the destination. Just like clipping those grape vines, your worst times become your best memories. I still remember the wave of happiness we shared when we found safety with the Red Cross. The marriage wasn't perfect, but we were still in love, and definitely in love with the Florida Keys.

We offered to donate to the Red Cross and they refused, as they were funded by the United Way. To this very day, I never refuse the United Way, and I will always remember their care and generosity, as well as the generosity of the local McDonald's, who fed us all for free.

When we arrived home, I was receiving congratulations from many people for leading the caravan. My wife got cheated—she had driven for twenty-four hours straight, essentially. I took the wheel and the adulation—it was like sitting down at a poker table, winning all the hands, and going home an hour later.

Still, we had made it home, and as crazy as it sounds, the trip was worth it. All of the craziness for an hour and half boat ride with our friends.

22

"But a man is not made for defeat.

A man can be destroyed but not defeated."

— Ernest Hemingway

I can't imagine writing a book about the Florida Keys and not including a story about fishing. I've always wanted to catch my "Hemingway fish," but the journey would take a lifetime.

In 1979, at thirteen years old, the water at G Marker was as clear as glass. The sun was hot, but back then we did not use sunscreen. There was a panfish on the end of my line and I was trying to reel it. I felt a large jerk on my rod and wham ! We were in a circle of boats and in the centre, there was a splash. What looked like a blacktip shark had jumped out of the water.

Whatever it was, it hit the water like a refrigerator from a third story apartment. My line broke and it was over: the panfish and the fish that took it was gone . The water returned to a calm state. It was the first time I swore in front of my parents.

Years later, I spent a lot of time fishing at Big Pine, mainly for food, but the big one always eluded me. I was never a fisherman, but I had some successes. Once I was on a fishing boat and hit a large school of flags (large yellowtail). When they hit the boat, the water at the back boiled with excitement. Usually, a large shark will eventually end the chum line.

I once had the opportunity to go for something big with my camp friends; Chicago Al, Captain Jim, and Rick. They were the cool guys in the camp, and I had finally scored a day on the boat with them.

Chicago Al had a biker image and he pulled it off for the most part, but we all knew he was a caring, sensitive guy on the inside. Everyone loved him. You knew he was the type of guy who always had your back. Once, during a camp altercation, he flew out of his motorhome yelling "Carl, man, I got your back." The offenders were removed from the family campground and life returned to normal. Jim drank loads of Pepsi and always warned me not to eat the brown acid. He was a Woodstock survivor. Rick owned a pontoon boat and was sure to always take people out on the ocean who didn't have access to a boat. Three great guys for sure.

On this particular day, we went out and the water was rough. I was terrified of getting seasick as I did not want to be "that guy." I had three pennies in my pocket and threw them in the ocean for good luck. I mused to myself that maybe today would be my day.

I sat in the back of the boat while the guys teased me for sitting in the "girlie seat."or the "pussy seat" . I was also the only guy with a neatly pressed T-shirt as my wife did the laundry. These guys were more seasoned, with rougher clothing. We were coming up dry and the speakers were blaring classic rock. Al always started with "Back Door Man." We were clowning around, dipping celery in peanut butter, and eventually a food fight erupted: we were basically children in adult bodies.

Just as things were getting out of hand, Captain Jim yelled, "grab the pole."

I was coached by these experienced guys and did fine overall. I was taught that if the fish runs the boat, put your rod in the water. Don't break the line. Reel, reel. My arms were sore, but I kept at it. After about fifteen minutes, a beautiful wahoo was at the side of the boat. The guys gaffed the fish and I was lucky as the great fish spit the lure out at the same time. The expert crew was instrumental in the landing of the fish. The wahoo hit the floor and its jaws were moving. I screamed like a high school cheerleader. I realized my error and yelled for someone to grab the club. Jim told me "we don't need a club. We got Al."

Just then, Chicago Al came from the front of the boat like William Wallace in the movie Braveheart. He held the fish in a headlock, then punched it like he was in a bar fight. Al was covered in wahoo slime but he had conquered this great fish. He let out a yell of victory.

The guys had a ritual I was uncomfortable with where you had to jump in the water and lap the boat in a victory swim. I have seen large sharks in those waters, so took some extra time to remove my watch, rings, and any other shiny objects.

I did jump in to conform. Despite being a city boy, I had caught my "Hemingway fish," and in my own way, I had conquered the Florida Keys. The next day, I nailed a large grouper bottom while fishing with my good friend Lou. Bottom fishing was where I belonged. These guys were men from the previous generation and had great character. True friends who would always have your back.

I'm indebted to them for my memories of the Florida Keys.

me and one legged George

The little red bus

Florida keys

me and Chicago AL

Sunsets and Granite Counter Tops

Florida keys

Florida keys

Florida keys

23

No matter how difficult the past, you can always begin again today.

– Jack Kornfield.

The first real cigar I smoked was an Ashton Prime Minister. This cigar, with a Connecticut wrapper, is exquisite. I liked cigars from the time I smoked my very first one. It is all about reflection.

We were off to Cape Cod. We had done twelve years in the keys. I remember going under a sign on our journey out there, Cape Cod: so many miles. I looked at the sign and for some reason it stuck in my mind.

We had an affordable holiday planned, and clearly, we took too many holidays; two timeshares, one in the spring and one in the fall, plus the Florida Keys. We basically lived better than many people who had lots of money. Our passion was road trips and that is one area where we were compatible. This vacation had taken its toll. We were doing well, and the cash flow could always pay a minimum balance. I had actually started another retirement fund and we had a house. We had something called equity, or so I thought.

We both worked hard. I was particularly exhausted, and our age difference was starting to be a problem (I was nine years older). I felt like I was raising a kid at times. I had convinced myself that a happy wife meant a happy life. Where I failed miserably was that I didn't appreciate "happy house, happy spouse." Husbands need to be happy, too. The truth is I had gained weight, I had allowed myself to be beaten into the ground. Actually, I was beating myself into the ground. I was exhausted and did not have much to give.

Cape Cod was beautiful and it wasn't crowded, as we were there one week after the season had ended. We scored nice weather. I recall walking with my pants rolled up and a shirt tied around my shoulders; like a Kennedy wannabe. I'm not sure who that guy was, but it wasn't me. We did a lot of sightseeing, but

I just could not keep up. I actually fell asleep. All I wanted was a glass of wine and a cigar, and to look out at the ocean. Our schedule was tight, and I never seemed to achieve this simple goal.

The whale watching was spectacular! We drove to a lake that legend said was filled with Indian tears, or something like that. On the last day, I lit that cigar and finally got my rest. Only too soon, the thought of our return trip made its way into my mind, and I couldn't enjoy the rest of my cigar.

You see, if you go out to dinner too often, you take the meal for granted. If you go out every two months, you really enjoy it. Too much of anything is not a good thing—except Florida, of course. I feared on the way home that the disconnect with my wife had grown too big. That year, I had just given up, and it must have been frustrating for my spouse. I ignored the signs. Twelve years of living large had caught up to us. People end a marriage when they want more. It's that simple. Rather than going into excessive details, it was over, and on my birthday the hammer came down. The marriage was over.

The house was sold and the typical arguments ensued. Much to our credit, we did it without lawyers. The bit of equity we had cleared most of our debt. We both walked away owing money, but what a ride we had.

Being a realtor and handling divorces: the patterns are very similar. I learned that clichés don't always help. However, there are two that stuck in my mind as significantly healing.

1. To get over being dumped, you have to get over yourself. I mean, you must realize that maybe the other person met someone who will make them happier. So if you are reading this, get over yourself.

2. The rear-view mirror is six inches wide for a reason. The windshield is four feet wide for a reason. Look forward. All this takes time. I truly believe that it sometimes takes as much as three to five years to process all the shit.

I moved into a rental apartment in a house that I had actually sold at one time, with Jamieson Irish whiskey as my chosen therapy. I was just existing and trying to get through my days. Each morning, it was a huge task just to get out of bed. I even saw a shrink and was diagnosed with situational depression. I had key friends rally to my side, while others abandoned me. I made it through Christmas, and I realized that it was the first big holiday without my wife. I realized that I loved her still, and that it was too late—she was gone, and she wasn't coming back.

By winter, I could tell that people were getting concerned about my state. My cousin needed a car taken to Florida, so when she sold her camper, she could drive her car to her boyfriend's. I would drive her car to Florida, and then fly home. I was getting some funds from the house sale, and despite my debt levels, I went to Florida. This time the Keys, my beloved Florida Keys, would save me. Since my cousins were there, I would have a place to stay. The Florida Keys had attracted my whole family at this point.

I arrived at the border in a car that didn't belong to me, and that's when the interrogation began. They asked me a million questions, searched my computer for illicit messages, and brought the drug sniffing dogs to check out the contents of the vehicle. I was there for hours, and answered question after question, by different border guards in different departments. I told them about my employment history, my marriage breakup, my current situation—nothing was off limits.

Finally, the last border guard handed me my passport and said, "You, sir, have had a very interesting life; I'm sorry your wife dumped you. The next time you come to the border, I hope you have a definite return date, and a beautiful blonde on your arm. You sure have been through a lot of stuff. Have a good vacation in the Florida Keys!"

I continued on my way and almost lost the car in a torrential downpour in Georgia when a car stopped just inches from my bumper. I was missing my designated driver—my spouse.

I had arrived in paradise, but I wasn't having any fun. I was spending too much time moping. I tried walking every day. Walking was the key. I walked down a long beach road, which I dubbed "Happy Road" because the walk among the mangroves by the ocean does wonders for the soul. When you are grieving, you are typically disconnected, even from nature. But seeing things that are familiar and that have brought you joy in the past sparks healing.

Still exhausted, and even tired of myself, I decided to do some open, or rustic, camping. There is a wonderful section of ocean front property for campers that doesn't have any electricity. I saw my old friend, One-eyed Chuck. He told me that he was sorry to hear about my wife. When I replied that I was fucked up, he poured me a 8 ounce brandy.

I gulped the first swig, and he said, "What the fuck is wrong with you? It's just a woman; they come and go like street cars." I told him that I would never meet another woman like my wife again. He said, "Why don't you talk to the one beside you, stupid?" There she was. She had beautiful, dark chestnut-brown hair, and the nicest smile.

She talked to me for a while and said, "OMG, you are a wounded animal." She was the right girl at the right time and we began a wonderful friendship. The last week of my holiday was the best, and things got better. When I said goodbye to her, I knew I had to see her again. I was still messed up because I was in love with my wife, but this girl was patient.

I flew home two days after she left; there was nothing for me at the camp. I knew that I had to go home and step up. I specifically remember stepping in a pile of snow and slush when I got home to Mississauga, Ontario and I instantly regretted not staying in Florida. I could easily have stayed another month. I sound entitled, but I cannot emphasize how much effort and labour went into seeing the Florida Keys.

This new woman was my saviour; my angel. Her heart was huge, and I just had to see her. I drove to New Hampshire two weeks later to see her. I hooked up with her and she said, "We're gonna party like rock stars." We did, and we had loads of fun.

After I got home and started to work, I realized that a long-distance relationship was not doable. I did not have the income or the time to do it. With a good friend like this, there will always be love. She called a few months later to check in on me. She could tell that I was still not doing that great, and she took me on a cruise to the Bahamas. My ex-wife found out and called me. She said, "Only you could meet someone and end up in the Bahamas." Near the end of the trip, I knew our fling was over, but not our friendship; that would last forever.

She moved on and met a wonderful man. We still have a yearly phone call, which I treasure. The funny thing is, when I drove out to see her, I recall going under the same Cape Cod sign that I had passed under with my wife. Life is funny. If someone had whispered in my ear, "Hey buddy, in a year's time you will be back visiting your girlfriend and going to the Bahamas," I would not have believed it! So, yes, life is fantastic.

I had a ways to go after this, but it was the turning point for me. The woman from the Florida Keys called me a year later and advised me that I had to be happy on my own. She said that I had to learn to travel on my own, and this great advice gave me the confidence to begin my journey to happiness. It took about five more years to find it, but I can honestly say that when you become grateful and understand how to manage your friendships and relationships, you will find happiness. It's just tragic that it took me fifty-two years to complete this life struggle.

I no longer feel the need to write *Man in the Basement* about man's struggle for happiness. It can be summed up in one word: GRATITUDE. Seek positive energy and manage negative energy.

The women I met in the Florida Keys saved me. The Florida Keys really had become my life.

24

Blindness separates people from things; deafness separates people from people.

— Helen Keller

I'm now down in the Keys, back on my feet, and life is good. My parents are no longer coming to the Keys; they decided it was time to travel less and enjoy life at home with the grandkids and great-grandkids. One of the things about an older clientele is people literally don't hear things.

On this wonderful spot called the Liar's Bench, just as when I was a child sitting with Chop Chop, people gather every morning for the camp coffee and talk about yesterday's catch, or the wind, and whether to fish the Gulf side or the Atlantic side.

Day 1 – After the initial hugs, I was back in my home. Things change, however, and I was smothered in my parents' shadow at first; they had been spending three months a year in Florida (the benefits of minimalism). My parents had been the kingpins of happy hour, and I was still taking knitting orders for my mom.

Day 2 – I was making new friends on Long Beach Road and at the Liar's Bench. People would say, "Did you really grow up here in this paradise? What a wonderful campground and resort! It is so well-run." I was now losing weight and focusing on my health because I always feel better in the Keys.

Day 3 – I was sitting on Liar's Bench when I heard from the other end of the bench, "What happened to John Stars?" One guy said he heard that John sold his house in Cayuga and rented a trailer. I laughed inside; I wanted to see how far this would go. I kept to myself for a change—I knew they had just rented an apartment.

Day 4 – The conversation and gossip continued. "Nope not true. I heard they sold the trailer and built a house in Cayuga."

At lunchtime, I came back from Winn Dixie on Big Pine with the "camp chosen drug" Carlo Rossi Vino, and a light lunch. I bugged Christa the front desk manager for a while. I talked with

Brenda the owner's daughter and had a Michelob back on the Liar's Bench, with a view of the water and palms. I reminisced about Chop Chop, Lou, my fishing partner, and all the wonderful people I met in my life. I had random thoughts of the past and present, and I realized I was now in "Keys speed"—slow—and I was happy.

A lady sat down. She realized I was John and Berit's son—in this place, I was still a kid in her eyes. She was excited about the connection, but I didn't remember her name. She was wondering how my parents were doing in Cuba, and why they quit coming to Big Pine Key. Cayuga had turned into Cuba. Later that day, I ran into another camp regular, and they asked how Canadians could get permission to build houses in Cuba.

The Liar's Bench has always added inches to the daily catch. The coffee and camaraderie are amazing. Even lonely people have family at this place—the Big Pine Key family. The Liar's Bench is quicker than the Internet at spreading information.

About Cuba: It is not uncommon to see refugees showing up in a homemade boat made of Styrofoam and pop bottles at Big Pine Key. Thousands of Cubans have risked their lives to land on the shores of Florida, Big Pine Key, in particular. Experiencing this makes me think of my father escaping Latvia. I am not afraid of socialism with democratic foundations, but I loathe communism. I rarely talk politics. I tell people I am a libertarian communist with liberal values and a conservative point of view with an environmental platform. This always shuts them up.

A year later I decided to go to Cuba, the first of three excursions to Cuba alone. Funny thing—it's ninety miles from Key West. Going to Cuba alone further strengthened my resolve, and one time when swimming in the ocean, I kept getting hammered by the waves and had trouble getting up. Life was sweet again. I was having fun and enjoying my own company, literally splashing in the water.

I toured a small town called Remedios, and I was horrified by the poverty. People would say that's typical of the tropics. True, I guess. But what wasn't typical is the buildings marked "K– 9 district" I actually witnessed a father selling his daughter in a dirt-floor home.

I went to Cuba three times, including visits to Havana and Santa Clara, where I attended the Che Guevara Mausoleum, and a celebration of the "freedom fighters" of the Castro revolution. It was my Forest Gump moment; I ended up in the square by accident listening to speeches that I could not understand. I felt like a czar in a Russian resort, while the peasants are working for daily food and no luxuries. Outside the gate. It was here that I realized true gratitude, and how lucky I had been to have such a great life. Anything from here on in was a bonus.

25

The past does not equal the future.

– Tony Robbins

As a young boy in the camp, I met a nice "nosy" lady from Canada, and I wasn't always the angel I make myself out to be. I never understood why people are so nosy—it's a pet peeve of mine. Much of my individualism philosophy was mind your business, do your own stuff, and take personal responsibility.

This lady's grandson had passed away, and I knew him—it was a tragedy. When I got married, she gave me a cowry shell, which I still have to this day.

She must have known me better than I realized because she said, "Congrats on the marriage, but don't have kids." She must have realized I might be a bachelor at heart, as she had known me in my adult years. She quipped, "Maybe the shell will bring you some luck some day." It's funny how every person in life touches you in some way. I felt she didn't endorse my wedding. She was a skeptic.

When it was time to sell my house, my neighbour knocked on the door and asked me to sell his home first. He was frustrated, as he could not secure employment, and life had kicked him in the shins. We decluttered his home and filled two budget bins with fifty years of junk. We converted one bedroom to a presentation room, as we were in the beginning of bidding wars.

I needed the commission, and the seller needed the money.

I walked into the bedroom and on the centre of the table was a cowry shell. I asked about the shell and he said, "that shell has always brought me good luck." The house sold for record price, and we both moved on with our lives.

Coincidence, I'm sure, that we both had cowry shells from Florida, but it's just funny how things tie together as you get older.

26

If you only work , than you really haven't lived

– carl stars

My childhood friend always said, "Don't work too hard. It's not you. Enjoy life." I had recently lost a good friend my age; he died of cancer. I had a long-time connection to him and his family in the Florida Keys. We were on my porch, and the last thing he said to me before he died was, "Carl, just hear the wind through the trees."

When he died, I went for a long bike ride—thirteen kilometres—which, for those who know me, was a one-off, for sure. On my return trip, a yellow butterfly followed me. The symbolism was predictable. Over the years living in Florida with an older crowd, I had lost many friends. I'm in my fifties, and I talk like a much older person. But I'm smart enough to know that the last twenty years goes by quickly. So learn to be happy and enjoy it. I hope in a small way this book helps someone.

I was in my office one day, and I opened a letter from another friend's father. It was a good-bye letter. I was not aware of how sick my friend's father was. I wish I had saved the letter. We exchanged a postcard every year—the same one—it said, "Buy low, Sell high." During an extreme financial challenge, he had lent me money, which I paid back. He always said "sympathy" was between "shit" and "syphilis" in the dictionary.

I was so absorbed in my work, I read his letter quickly, and never paid it the respect it deserved. To this day I wish I had saved the letter. Upon hearing of his death, I remarkably remembered the letter and its contents. You can learn from people even after they die. He died on a tropical island with a cigarette and a drink in his hand, on a balcony overlooking the ocean. What a way to go. Turned out he was something of a philanthropist, and gave a lot of money away, but he did it under the radar. He was a good man.

A year later I headed to Sarasota, Florida to visit his son. He had found God and was actively debating my atheist beliefs. Many of his arguments were good. He mentioned the human eye, which has thousands of nerves—how could that be created out of dust and goo? And you are telling me there is not a creator? The visit was great, but very different for me. It was time to leave Sarasota and head to the Keys. This would be my last trip for a while; I had completed my college courses and was beginning a new career. I knew it was time to grow up and work; after all, I was fifty-one.

Some time later, I was back in the Keys again—cigars, rum, palm trees, and friends. It was going to be a longer vacation this time; twenty-eight days. I was on my feet financially but was under tremendous pressure from family and friends; they said I was just too careless, and I should think about skipping Florida for a while and get more established. I had money in the bank, but real estate was somewhat slow in February. It was time. I was more on my own; my parents and many of our mutual friends had moved on. I had noticed that I was treated differently, socially, without a wife. We tend to think in couples and only a single person understands this. But I enjoyed my limited social contact. I would bridge fish with the locals who appeared to be lower income. They were always more grateful and happier than the rich people on the canal. Economic rules are even the same in the campground. I would give them most of my daily catch, keeping a few for myself. I would return around four o'clock, grill my fish by the ocean, have a cigar and rum, and look out on the same view I used to look at with my friend, Vietnam George. My lifetime had been in this place. I still got some social invitations, but for fun I would go visit the pirates and hippies over in open camping.

My four mile walk on "happy road" by the mangroves was a daily treat, and I was informed by many of the older campers that I was far too young to be there in my late forties/early fifties, not working. It was like I was breaking the rules or committing a crime. **Where does it say you have to work like a dog your whole life before you are entitled to enjoy a sunset?**

Whenever I hear a gust of wind through the trees I still think of my good friend who passed away. On one particular day I was walking down the road, and I had turned a corner. I appreciated the life I had, and the only constant all the way through was the Florida Keys. I was actually thinking about my friend in Sarasota, his father, and those religious beliefs so many of my friends have. I know that, as humans, we are weak and we look for something to hang on to. I thought to myself, *if there is a god, I want a sign right now*. Just then, a gust of wind moved a palm tree violently, and I thought of my good friend who had passed. Oddly enough, the ocean and mangroves were dead calm—how on Earth did this palm tree move? I'm sure there are many scientists who can explain this. I contemplated whether I would even tell this story in the book, as many of my friends would question my sanity.

I have often questioned why we have to believe blindly? That day I laughed to myself about the mystery of life. I said now would be a time to get a "sign," as if the palm tree wasn't enough. I took about ten more steps with my head down, as I was in deep thought. I looked up and almost ran into the friend's mother who had passed that I was just thinking about. I had moved from atheist beliefs to at least recognizing that there is an energy out there. I felt, late in life, that I had achieved some sort of synchronicity. I have not analysed this much but it felt so real.

A couple of years later, I visited my childhood friend from the Keys, and life had gone full circle. They told me about their son, who had died at birth. My friend's wife had shared the story with their neighbour the day before I was there and a hummingbird showed up. The same thing happened a few years earlier when she visited her sons grave: a hummingbird showed up. I had dropped in for a few Budweisers—we drank American beer from our Florida Keys upbringing—and I bravely told my story about my walk down Happy Road. I felt a connection with my childhood friend and when our stories were over, we had a quiet moment. The tree in the rear yard moved with a incredibly strong gust of wind. Everything else was calm. "just to hear the wind through the trees." We smiled and sipped our beer quietly. There was an understanding about how unique life is. We had both grown up in the Keys, and we had both achieved happiness on very different paths.

27

10000 Swedes ran through the weeds,

chased by one mad Norwegian.

– Norske Folklore

I was in the Big Pine Key campground by the ocean, doing what I do best—nothing. A French tourist walked by my campsite, "Hiyah, nice place here, eh?" Then he corrected himself and said, "There are nicer places in da world." I looked at him, drew on my cigar, exhaled, and said, "Yes, maybe, but I don't want to go there."

It may seem narrow-minded; I have travelled through some of Europe, half of Canada, and many areas of the Unites States, but I always end up in Florida, and in particular, the Florida Keys.

I was by the pool—Big Pine Key has a resort-style swimming pool and wonderful lofts you can rent, so it is much more than a campground—and I was reading a book about Che Guevara. A French woman walked by and said, "You are reading a book about Che, my hero. Where are you from?"

I answered, "Canada," and added, "Che and Castro killed a lot of people." She abruptly replied, "So did Americans in Iraq." I smiled politely and successfully avoided a political debate. I had clearly interacted with the husband and wife.

They probably said the Canadian guy was closed-minded and doesn't know anything about the world. They would have been horrified to learn I drank the unofficial camp wine, Carlo Rossi California Red.

Home again, I was thinking about another trip to the Keys. I logged on to Facebook, and there was a message: "Are you Stars, son of Berit Stapplefeldt?" I replied with hesitation. After a brief exchange, I realized I was talking to my second cousin. I was skeptical. I mean, Facebook reunites lost dogs with owners, and if a relative dies, you can tell a whole bunch of people quickly, but was this person real? We exchanged several photos, and she sent me pictures of her mother's apartment with my relatives' pictures on the wall. Somehow, with the family ties, and even though my mother was corresponding with her mother, I was not fully aware of my second cousin. I have second cousins in Toronto I haven't seen in four years, and these things happen.

My second cousin did not look like me at all, thank goodness. We exchanged several emails, and I was fearful I would be invited to come to Norway. If I went to Norway, I would miss the Florida Keys. But this time, I felt a strong bond over the Internet, and I realized that I had the money for the flight and a twelve day stay, so why not go for it.

My cousin picked me up with a friend in Oslo after a tiring night. I started the next day with brunch, with all the foods I was raised on—smoked salmon, egg, herring, and the list goes on. My cousin was driving me to my mother's hometown and she got lost; I discovered that she has no sense of direction, my problem too. My driving has even cost me relationships. She started playing B.B. King and Eric Clapton's *Riding with the King* while, under my sweater, I was wearing a B.B. King shirt.

We were at a Viking ship museum having a drink when we both jumped. A bee had came down and attacked—we discovered that we are both allergic to bees. I saw a Viking ship with a serpent head, and that was the missing piece to the puzzle for the tattoo I had been mentally planning for years.

We stayed up and talked till three a.m. I learned that she smokes, and much to my surprise, she sits like my mother, and has my grandmother's sense of humour. I met her son and he is exactly like my nephew (their girlfriends could even be twins). It was an alternate universe. I met her mom, and it was like seeing my grandmother again; I mean, it's family.

My cousin's brother—who was also called Hans, like my brother—was not physically like my brother, but their personalities were similar—they both seemed to tolerate talking about work or normal pleasantries, but it was exhausting for them.

I was raised with Latvian culture, which is more eastern European than Norwegian culture. While I do have some Norwegian traits, I fed off the Latvian side too much. However, my life struggle of working hard and slowing down was a combination of my father's side and my mother's side. The Norwegian side is where the ambition comes from.

I was discovering my mother's hometown, and a fish market in her father's town. In Tønsberg, the shrimp sandwiches in the restaurant by the water were to die for. We had drinks and celebrated our last night. I looked around the restaurant and my cousin and I knew right then and there how much Norwegian was also in my personality, compared to the Latvian. A bond was formed for life and my cousin and I message often. I sometimes think about her, and then I get a message. We deal with our family "issues" in the same way, and a bond has formed. I have finally found my people.

Oddly enough, we exchanged photos recently—her dining room table had a box of Kleenex, a candle, and a serving tray—exactly the same as mine—we were and are kindred souls.

I then travelled to Latvia and discovered my father's hometown. The Russian driver I hired gave me a tour for the day. His name was Victor. I was fortunate to discover Riga, and I realized how strong the influences of my upbringing were. I left with a clear understanding of my father's escape route from the Russians, and we can be thankful to Sweden for taking in my father's family.

Riga, without a doubt, was the most beautiful city I have ever seen, and the boat tour on the interior River Daugava was exhilarating. I saw a sailboat with the last name Stars on it (not a common name; a relative, I wondered?). I flew into the Ukraine and back to Canada. I was happy I went to Latvia, and I was anxious to tell my Latvian cousins in Toronto all about my adventures. I almost felt guilty because I missed my family in Norway terribly for the two days I was in Latvia.

Finally understanding what I am and who I am were the missing pieces to the puzzle, as happiness had been achieved, and with gratitude every day going forward, it would also be appreciated.

Of course, my original thought from seven years prior when in Big Pine Key was to get a tattoo of a Norwegian Viking ship floating on braided water (Namejs Latvian ring). That was achieved upon my return to Canada. Yes, mid-life crisis, maybe, but it is a daily reminder of my family, who I am, and who I had become.

28

Life is truly a boomerang. What you give, you get.

– Dale Carnegie

A few years back, I had my final drink with a friend in Burlington Ontario. He had been rich in his life, and he had been poor. He was a modern version of *Death of a Salesman*—still using old clichés like, *You can't make an omelette without breaking an egg*. We had a cigar and a shot of rum—he always drank single shots. His Polish father had taught him to pour an ounce at a time to minimize the damage.

He exclaimed, "If I knew I could be this happy, I would have lived here thirty years ago! My god, man; this place is perfect and what a view of the lake!" He was renting an apartment.

Carl Stars

I was helping him with his final real estate offer, and a few days later, he was dead. I wouldn't take his money, but he offered me a bottle of port. I declined, hoping I would see him again and have a drink another time, but he died before that could happen. At his funeral, there was an ex-girlfriend and two ex-wives grieving over his coffin. That is how you know he did something right.

A light bulb turned on in my head, and I knew it was time to get out of the city and live life on my terms. My friend who had just died was very happy to the end. I wanted to be that happy as well. I rented an apartment and it turned out to be the same apartment I had lived in twenty-five years before and hated.

A full circle of life had happened. I was miserable when I left this building, as I pursued everything you could imagine. Now fully content in life, I had a small apartment, affordable rent, a great job, lots of cashflow, lots of golf games, and many sunsets over the river. My cost of living had dropped by sixty percent and life was so darn easy, I could not keep a straight face.

I had finally found peace. No more excessive drinking; I was investing in a future that might not come. I was living for today and only today. I found new joy in doing things that brought happiness to others and to myself. I was now living a life filled with gratitude. To many of you, these may be just words. With the Internet, we read these words daily, yet we don't fully understand them. I was no longer chasing granite countertops, but I was definitely chasing sunsets.

I went out to the balcony and lit up a cigar. I laughed at the aging process; I was always an old soul. One girl I broke up with had a real good line: "You're a nice guy, but I'm not ninety." I was fifty-four at the time, but could easily have been sixty-four, or seventy-four, for that matter. I was sitting in my favourite chair looking at the beautiful river; the fall leaves had covered the ground. I was within a stone's throw of being my grandfather. The sun hit the river with the same sheen I had noticed walking downtown on the way to the Christmas parade when I was young.

The temperature was the same, and winter was around the corner. This year, in a pandemic, many people are struggling, and yet I am thriving. Life is funny, with all its twists and turns. There will be more good times, more dreams, and maybe more love.

I had come off the previous day's high—the golf courses were closing for the winter, and my friends and I had managed to squeeze in one more round. It was an absolute blessing to have that day, and the connection to nature had brought me happiness. It was a perfect way to end the season. One person in our group was fighting cancer, and my admiration for him playing golf between chemo treatments was huge. I was thinking about my new girlfriend, work, my retirement fund (yes, I started another one), what I was going to have for dinner, and the beautiful river in front of me, flowing peacefully by.

My mind drifted off to the Florida Keys and all the memories I have. It's funny that I found happiness when I finally learned to live life on my own terms; some learn this quick, some learn it slow, and some never learn it.

I put the cigar out in the ashtray, then reached over and grabbed it at the last minute for one more smoke; life tasted sweet.

Looking at the bright sun and the river, I thought about how great it was to be alive. How funny it is to truly understand that gratitude is the key to happiness. Getting up from the chair and going in to my apartment that I once hated, I turned and looked at the Grand River one more time. I only saw beauty.

I was thinking, it sure would be nice to go back to the Florida Keys again one day.

The end

Printed in the USA
CPSIA information can be obtained
at www.ICGtesting.com
LVHW041222111223
766048LV00001B/93